Short Stories, Essays and Exercises On the Path to Self Discovery

ISBN 978-0-9796507-1-0

Introduction

The mind is a powerful ally for us to live in this world. However given absolute control of our lives, it becomes a silent tyrant.

Indeed, there is no master more ruthless, no jungle more wild, and no fire more fierce and consuming than the reactive mind. Therefore the battlefield of the mind is the only one we have to conquer, the only prison we have to walk out of, and then we can realize we have always been free. Freedom is the true nature of our being.

This book is a collection of Short Stories, Essays and Exercises which the author wrote over the years as a record of observations on her own journey towards finding the authentic Self.

The author wishes to inspire the readers into self inquiry by incorporating her experiences in all the work and distilling those experiences for everyone to try.

It is meant to be light reading rather than a textbook.

"The greatest politeness is free of all formality,
perfect conduct is free of concern,
perfect wisdom is unplanned,
perfect love is without demonstrations,
perfect sincerity offers no guarantee." The way of Chuang Tzu by
Thomas Merton

Table of Contents

How to Perfect Your Faith

There are so many entries on faith in the bible

This is my favorite definition of faith in the bible. "Faith is the assurance of things hoped for, the conviction of things not seen" [Hebrews 11:1 KJV], and my favorite story, that of the Centurion whose slave was ill and who said to Jesus, "Command that he gets well and it is done."

Indeed every time I go back to that story I am reminded to reexamine my faith and yet, every time I go back it was always a time when I had perfected faith by surrender that miracles occurred. My ego always wants me to control how things will go, from the most mundane to the greatest challenges.

God does not test our faith. There is no need to do so. We create all these little dramas in our lives to experience something that we may grow. Hard as I try, I cannot imagine a punitive God.

I will illustrate this with a story. Once there was a man who had always been righteous. He never did anything wrong, did his duties well, and generally was very happy. His passion was designing ocean faring vessels, from the simplest to the most elaborate.

He was content with his work. It was how he honored God for every ship that he built, he first offered to God. Because he built ships, he traveled a lot and when he thought he had already worked enough, he decided to retire and simply concentrate on his volunteer work. He can now devote more time to helping others, not monetarily but with his time.

Although he has been quite successful, he lived simply, had plenty of good friends, and at sixty years of age, he had amassed a great fortune he planned to donate to charity when he passed on. He had never been married, nor had he fallen in love with anyone.

One day, while visiting a long time friend who had invited him to dinner, someone knocked on the door. As his friend was cooking dinner and could not leave the kitchen he asked the man to please open the door, and there she was, young and beautiful and with the most soulful eyes he had ever seen. He thought he was dreaming for his heart jumped, he felt it.

He thought she was an angel that just dropped from the heavens.

The woman turned out to be the daughter of the neighbors across and she had come to ask if the paper was delivered that day because her parents did not get theirs. They were introduced and from then on he decided that this is the woman he wanted to marry.

So he courted her with flowers and presents and everything else he could think of. Generally she was very nice and kind hearted with him, but he knew she did not love him, not the romantic way. And the man got very frustrated, for there was nothing and no one he desired most.

One night after another frustrating night he turned to God. He was in his living room and he said out loud, "Why God, must you put this desire in my heart when you would not grant me her love. I have never asked You for anything and I am always grateful for what you have given me. I am asking you now! "

And he wept,like an abandoned child for his pain was so great, and afterwards he fell asleep.

And an angel swept his spirit and took him to a place which seemed to float in the clouds and God was there.

And God waved His hand and there appeared another place and the man saw himself with this woman he loved. They were married and had children, but the woman fell in love with another man and she tried to leave him.

And in his anger, he took a gun and shot his wife and her lover and his children saw this and he was filled with remorse and he shot himself as well.

And God said to him, "Because you have always been faithful to me, I can grant you your wish and make her fall in love with you.

But behold, what I showed you is what will happen in a few years, and that is a consequence of my intervening on your behalf, right now.

Do you wish it?"

And the man woke up and behold it was a dream, and he understood why God did not want to grant him his wish. And he knelt and prayed in earnest, and thanked God for his dream.

He decided that it was best for him to forget the woman so he buried himself in charity work far away from where the woman lived, and did not visit the woman again. He told his friend the woman's neighbor that he would be away and will not be visiting him for a while.

A few years passed and when he came back he had totally lost interest in the woman and he visited his friend again.

When he arrived, there was somebody there with his friend. A woman! Oh but this woman looked so much like the woman he first fell in love with, but was older and also her eyes were different. It was full of compassion and kindness he could almost feel that the woman was pure and with a great love for God.

And his friend spoke and said "Please meet Mary, the other daughter of my neighbors across. Mary was in a nunnery for a long time but decided that her place was not in the nunnery but in serving various charities, and I thought you could use her help with your various charities.

And the man knew that this woman was what God reserved for him.

The Caged Bird

Once there was a man and he had a bird that could sing, for it was a magical bird. Indeed, its songs were beautiful, and every time he felt sad, the bird would sing to him and he would feel better and he was happy.

And when he left for work he would leave the cage door open and a small opening in the window so that the bird could come and go as it pleased.

The bird did fly away to meet with other birds when the man was gone but it always came back before he came home and he would always see the bird asleep with the cage door closed, for it flew into the heavens when he was gone and although it could sing, it could not speak to him about the worlds that it visited.

And even if it could not speak, it enjoyed listening to the man telling it of his day.

And every once in a while, he did tell the bird of his day. But he was busy in the outside world, and he neglected the bird. Sometimes he would not come home and there would be no food or water for the bird, but the man assumed that it could get nourished on its own, after all, it was a magical bird.

But it was not the water nor the food that nourished the bird, it was the love that came with the food when the man fed it that kept it alive in this physical world.

One day, the bird did not come back and the man was very sad. For he knew it was not coming back, and for the first time he realized that it was not the food that nourished the bird. And he knew it left because although he loved it, he neglected it. He was mesmerized by the sights and sounds and all the things that are in this material world. And the man was sad and longed for the bird to come back.

And then one day, he met a woman. And he knew it was the bird. And the woman told him "It is I. I flew into the heavens and I was not coming back, but your love brought me back, in another form, so you would never be alone again, for I will always be with you until we are released from these bodies, and we can fly into the heavens, together."

The Education of a god

Once upon a time a pious King and his wife wished for a son to rule the kingdom wisely, for they loved the people.

The being who chose to be born to the King and Queen was a god, whose education was not yet perfected. He chose to be born as the son to perfect his education for he wished to experience life as a human being again, and so he was born and raised as the future ruler of the kingdom.

While he was being raised as a human being and temporarily forgetting he is a god who has not fully realized himself, everyone was watching him, including all of the teachers of a council. Thus he learned not only everything required for a future king, but his teachers in human form taught him about other worlds as well. But as he took the form of a human being, he was thus limited by the form and everything it entails.

The council which monitors the education of the young Prince agreed to test him on his 21st birthday and the king and the queen was informed by the sages in the palace that as a king who would rule the kingdom someday he must be wise, and so the test was prepared. The King and Queen agreed to visit a neighboring kingdom as guests of that kingdom for a period enough for the sages in the palace to do the testing.

The queen was not happy but agreed to leave her son in the care of the sages and the palace staff.

On his 21st birthday, the palace was opened to everyone and among the many guests he was to choose a few people whom he has no knowledge about and allow them to stay in the palace with him for a week following a three week celebration where everyone was invited.

As part of the test, he is to make all of his decisions on his own without counsel from anyone.

The celebration was joyous. The subjects were very pleased with the young Prince, and as he was raised by wise parents they knew that he too would rule wisely.

Thus came the time when the guests he had chosen were to stay in the palace for a week, and the young Prince was to choose two from among his many guests and the two he chooses will live in the palace with him as part of his counsel.

The ten guests he chose were housed in the many rooms in the palace and wined and dined with the Prince, and during the week, everyone became his friend. At the end of the week they were to bid the Prince goodbye and go back to their old life.

The first one thought that since he is now the friend of the future king, he could take whatever he wanted from the palace. Thus he chose a golden goblet and took it with him along with a few gold coins. He had no intention of coming back to the palace, he would go to a far, far away place and enjoy his life.

He would be a wealthy man. Thus with the help of two other guests he was able to conceal the stolen goods from everyone else when they left the palace, and they all agreed to meet in one place to share the loot. Thus for the sake of gold, he abandoned the friendship of the future King. As he was before, as he is now.

The second one was a Brahmin, like the King, and he thought he would just enjoy the company of the future king. Wealth meant nothing to him as he too was quite wealthy, and he expected to be invited as one of his counsel and enjoy life as the Prince's counsel, but although he did not covet the prince's wealth, he had contempt for the Prince whom he thought foolish. He could then influence the future king's decision and rule behind the throne. But the Prince could see through this plot and thus dismissed this man as well.

All others thanked the future King and were ready to leave but the one question remained. What to do with the thief and his two cronies.

The future king knew of the theft, and at first he was really angry that his friendship was betrayed. The punishment for theft was cutting the hand of the thief, but as he stole from the future king after having been invited to wine and dine with him the laws of the kingdom required that the three thieves be first tortured in a chamber and it would be at the mercy of the king to put them to death.

As the king and queen were absent, it is now up to the future king to decide their fate.

All but one of the guests said the thief and his partners be beheaded immediately. One, said, "O future king. This man and his partners stole from you. What harm has he done? You have more riches than any one of us in the kingdom, for you will someday inherit the kingdom. I beg you let him go with mercy."

The sages and teachers awaited his decision, for in it lies the key to his freedom as a god. Full knowledge of his being. At last the future King spoke. "Let them go and double what they stole from me, for I have more riches than anyone. And if they use it to do another human being a kindness, then perhaps someday they themselves will realize honor."

And with this he realized the god that he is, and that his earthly travel was no more than a wish he had, and that his home was away from this place. And in that moment he exchanged places and faces with the merciful guest who was a gypsy, and away he left as one of the other guests.

And the gypsy conceived himself to be the prince. And the Prince bid the other Brahmin to stay with him in the palace as a reflection of his own humanity.

When the King and Queen arrived they decided that it was time to crown the new King. And thus the king ruled wisely until his death and he had many wives and children and the kingdom flourished when the king was wise, and declined when the king was foolish, but the earth and its inhabitants remained.

And the god, came and went as he wished, now a woman, now a man, now a pauper, now a prince, just to visit the place where he had learned the meaning of kindness and of love and of justice, for at other times, he sat at the council in a place that most ordinary humans cannot conceive.

It was a point where space and time and objects, even galaxies, were created and uncreated at will.

The Sage and The Sorcerer

Once there was a very powerful magician. He was so powerful that he could command the forces of nature to his bidding. As such he ruled the world, for whomever he came in contact with would fall under his spell.

And he made the world his playground and he toyed with everything and everyone, until one day, he encountered a monk. And this monk would not fall under his spell. So the magician followed the monk into the forest determined to show this monk the extent of his powers.

When the monk sat in meditation, the magician summoned the wind to be so strong that the trees swayed and fell all around the monk, but the monk was deep in meditation and did not open his eyes.

The magician, determined to wake the monk from his deep meditation summoned the wind once more and this time told it to bring heavy rains with it. And so it rained really hard, but a circle around the monk was formed and lo and behold, the land around the monk was dry!

The magician then got really angry, thinking that the monk sat still undisturbed. And the magician conjured a spell to create fire and threw it into the monk, and a great fire engulfed the forest and the other inhabitants in the surrounding villages flee in terror, but the fire did not reach the monk, and he sat still undisturbed.

And the magician then became really angry and created thunderstorms and hurled lightning at the monk, but the lightning boomeranged back into the space where it came from, and the magician thought he had met another magician more powerful than himself.

The magician then bowed a bow of obeisance to the monk and said, "O monk, you are a more powerful magician than I, and I would be grateful if you showed me your secrets and in exchange I will also teach you everything I know and we can rule the world together.

For I can conjure the most powerful spells that heads of States, Kings and Queens bow to me if I wish."

And the monk opened his eyes and told the magician "I will teach you the secret of all secrets, and know that you can not deceive me as you have already seen that though you may command the forces of nature to do your bidding, I am immune to it. Would you agree?"

The magician felt a terror that he had not felt before and he knew that this monk was telling the truth, for he himself had witnessed it, and so he said to the monk "If you teach me the secret I promise to be obedient to you and I will only do as you bid and I will relinquish all of my powers to you." And so the powerful magician said, in truth.

The monk then said "Look into your heart, for it is where the secret of secrets is buried."

And the magician looked into his heart and lo and behold he saw his past lives and how he had become greedy of power and how he enjoyed the power he wielded over others, and he also remembered all the compassion and the kindness of the people in his past lives and the present, and he wept.

For in his heart he felt love for these people he had left behind in search of power which he now possessed. And in his heart he wished to be back where he was before, a simple ascetic."

And the monk said, now look again, and behold the magician saw that the monk was in his heart and the face of the monk was his own, and that the monk he was talking to was gone. And then he heard the voice of the monk that said "I am you, you had simply forgotten, having fallen into the world of illusion you yourself created.

And because you had shown humility and compassion, you have now known the secret of all secrets, which is love. Go now and be free."

And he went back to the village where he came from, stripped of all his magical powers, and he sought to teach the people instead, the meaning of compassion and of love.

The Sleeping god

Once upon another universe, there existed and still exist a group of very powerful beings and they created and threw away universes as their game, and their only game was who could create the most beautiful sight and create the most beautiful harmony, and because they were not embodied, they only exchanged harmonic oscillations. And they would create and destroy at will.

Because they were all powerful they agreed that those who lost a game had to be punished, and the punishment was "To forget". As they were each as equally as powerful, the only way to overcome another, the one that lost a game would be for those who were participating in the game to "encompass" the one who lost the game, and to make the game more interesting, they created a universe of penalties.

Because all of them created the universe of penalties, not a single one of them can undo what the other beings did, but each one could undo his own contribution and use it as a portal to go back to where they came from.

As part of the game they could replicate each other indefinitely so the beings freely replicated themselves and to make the game more interesting, the replicates would forget that they were replicates because each was fully endowed with the powers of the original source.

Now the penalty universes were what we read in myths...the magical universe was one of them and the legend of Merlin was in fact a memory of those times.

In the magic universe there were two beings that were hurled there by mistake and they were more powerful than the rest and so the other magicians connived with each other and bound the two and planned to hurl them in the prison planet where they would forget everything. Everything.

One of them got out but did not want to abandon the other, so it too was hurled and bound and sent to the prison planet called Earth. And as prisoners they were given bodies as part of their punishment and when one body disintegrated, another one was given and so it went on and on for thousands of years.

But because the two beings had a "memory" of each other they would eventually meet each other after rebirth, lifetime after lifetime but still they did not remember who they were. But the spirit remembers. Their souls had a memory of each other .

And sometimes one would have the body of a man and the other a woman and they would fall in love and be caught up in the programming from previous in between lives and eventually they would end up parting. But their dreams were always connected with each other.

But lifetime after lifetime one of them would remember more and more and until one lifetime the being in the body of a woman vowed to solve every childhood dream she had which did not make sense: by will and by discipline. aThey did meet again and she knew,it was him!

But he did not believe and dismissed it to the highly imaginative mind of the other. And she tried and tried and tried and tried to tell him, and although he felt a deep love for her his programming was in so deep it would take several more lifetimes for him to wake up.

And although the being in the woman wishes deeply that it could depart this prison planet for she has fully awakened, it remembers the time of myth and magic when the other refused to leave her. And she would come back again, for the other, until the other fully remembers the he too, is a god. A sleeping god.

Waking Up from a Dream

Once there was a boy who dreamt that he was a prince in a kingdom not visible to the humans. The visible and the invisible worlds were superimposed with each other but there was a thin film that permeated everything but it separated the two worlds from each other.

The inhabitants of the two worlds could not cross unless something from the world where one comes from was given up.

The boy had two guardians, and the guardians told him the truth of his being, and that is, he was the son of the Great One. His guardians were there and played with him, and sometimes they would rearrange the stars in the heavens at night, sometimes they would make new galaxies, and sometimes they would go to the depths of the ocean and play with the fishes, and every time they came back to the surface of the earth, the boy would ask, where are the others? Why am I alone with you? And guardians always told him that soon they would tell him.

One day when the guardians were about and the boy was left alone and he was looking at the water and it reflected his face, but it also reflected many beings, creatures that he never saw before. When he asked the guardians if they made those creatures, they said it was time to tell him.

"Everything and everyone that you saw emanated from the Great One. You are a part of the Great One, as we are also parts of the Great One. The creatures that you saw were all created in an instant, for the Great One wishes to forget that it is alone and therefore made many copies of it with different characteristics. In truth, it is just itself playing just as you and we play. What you saw was the earth with the humans. From our world we can see them but they cannot see us. There is a great barrier that separates the two. The law created by the Great

One does not allow crossing over to the other side without sacrificing the attributes of one world. Every human being that you saw is related to you as we are related to you. We are all parts of the Great One.

And the boy looked at everything that was happening in the other world, and he wondered why humans were acting the way they did fighting over things when in fact they could have the thing that they covet if only they remembered, for he himself could create anything just by thinking it.

The guardians told him that when they crossed to the other world, they had forgotten who they were for they had drank the nectar of illusion. And the boy wanted so much to bring the others back to his world, but the guardians told him that the only way to do that was to live with them and show them the truth, and it could only be done if the boy himself drank the nectar of illusion which would make him forget that he was a divine being.

And the boy said, "I will drink the nectar of illusion, but I will remember who I AM so that I can bring everyone back to this world where they belong ."

And the guardians said "The secret will be buried in your heart for surely you will forget who you are when you drink the nectar, but every time you learn a human lesson and show compassion to the other beings a part of it will be revealed to you until you remember completely who you are.

But in the other world, you will be bound by the laws of that world, and you will have a body that will not last forever and you will think that time is real, and you will experience hunger and thirst, and every other human emotion and you will have to discover, for in the other world it is through suffering that they learn so to be born in the other world is to suffer.

The great illusionist lured them to play on earth saying they will experience what it was like to be ordinary and one by one they forgot. Every once in a while, someone will have a glimpse of this world, but the attraction of the other world to a human being is so strong that they always go back, back to earth "to play" the games of hide and seek, .

On the other hand when you have transcended everything, and finally wake up to the truth of your being, you will be able to guide others back into this world.

And the boy drank the nectar of illusion, and he too took the human form, and he experienced everything that a human being experienced.

Once he was born as a great warrior and he conquered half of the earth, and he discovered that it was the conquest that he liked, and he got tired of it. At another time he was born as a great artist and he loved making beautiful things and he continued to create great works of art. And he discovered that the adulation of the patrons was not enough.

Another time he was born a great scientist and he showed the world a different way of thinking, but this too was not enough. Sometimes he would be born rich, sometimes he would be born poor, and he discovered that it made no difference. Then he learned about kindness, for every time he loved, he was a little kinder.

And every time he showed compassion a part of the secret was revealed to him until finally, after many years of rebirth, he was born a sage, and he inspired others to follow his path, and he did this again for several lifetimes, spanning the history of mankind.

And at last when he had transcended everything, he went back to the other world, and he saw that some of his brothers were there, but some of them were still left in the earthly world. So the boy decided that he would come back over and over again until each and every one of his brothers realized the truth of who they were, but this time, because he had already known the truth of his being from having experienced life as a human being, he could choose whom to be born to and where.

His birth was no longer a random event which was a consequence of a previous life.

And the boy woke up when he heard his mother's voice saying "Wake up o Prince, for the shower awaits and the school bus does not wait." And his mother came into his room and kissed him on the head and said "Time to wake up. Did you have a good dream?" as she pulled off the covers from his eyes.

And the boy looked into his mother's eyes and thought with utmost kindness "This woman who is my mother in this lifetime has been reborn so many times but is still bound by the limited thinking of humans. Yes, it is time to wake her up." The boy pulled the cover back over his head and said to his mother "I'll get up in five minutes."

And the boy went back to sleep for five more minutes on earth time.

And the Great One smiled and the sun rose from the horizon. It was just another day in paradise.

Essays

Some of the Essays here were originally published in EzineArticles between June 30, 2007 and November 14, 2009.

Article Source:

http://ezinearticles.com/expert/Melinda_M._Sorensson/106714#

They were edited for inclusion in the present publication.

Essence

My son and I share a passion for history. I must admit that as I write this, he knows more about it than I do. I look at history in terms of people, what drives them.

I love old houses. They have character. They are imprinted with the signature of the previous owners. I love the house that we live in. It is perfect for the four of us. My son, my two dogs and myself.

The house that we live in is quite ordinary. It has three bedrooms and two full baths and a half bath outside. I always wondered why there is a bathroom outside of the main house. One of my previous colleagues told me that it was probably constructed for the help who landscaped the yards. It does have a very big backyard. It took me two years to find this house and it was as perfect then as it is now. I had to change a couple of things here and there, but the yard is pretty much the same except for the addition of a water fountain.

Oh except one of the trees fell off when hurricane Lily passed. On it's stump I placed a concrete statue of the buddha. This one is unusual because it is a smiling buddha and the hands are not folded in a meditation posture. It is as if the buddha is just enjoying the traffic of all kinds of birds taking baths in the fountain, the squirrels that tease the dogs and, one day, even a snake. All part of the dance of life in my backyard.

The couple who used to live here are retired and they did a terrific job of landscaping the property. Even now, when azaleas are in bloom, ours is the only home surrounded by magnificent colors in our neighborhood which also an older neighborhood. I can only remember one house that seems to change owners unusually frequently for as long as we have lived here. Most of the residents on the houses lining the street are either retired or working at home, so on any one weekday, the cars are parked on the carport as if it were a weekend.

The pine tree in the backyard is the tallest on the street. I can see it as long as I am on the same street. It serves as a beacon to me.

The flowering plants that continue to give us flowers were planted by the previous owners. I am always grateful for the generosity of spirit of the previous owners for leaving us this gift. I can tell they loved the land as I do now.

That is the history of this house for me. That is what I will remember when I either move away someday or die. I wonder how it was for the people who built it? I wonder how my son will remember it when he goes to college? He always thought it too small. No swimming pool. No tennis court. Not a place for big parties. For me, it is perfect. Small enough that I know where he and the dogs are at any one time even when I am at work on my computer.

I will always remember this house as the house where I found the most peace. When I pass on the ownership of this house to someone else, I wonder what they would change and what they would keep? What kind of signature will they leave? I hope that at least they will keep the bananas and the lemon tree and the dogwoods that I planted. Oh and I will leave them the buddha on the stump and the water fountain as my gift, just like the previous owners left calla lilies and african daisies and the enormous fig tree as their legacy to the future occupants of the land.
For the land remains. The house may change, the occupants do change,but the land will always keep a record of the life that was there.

While Scrubbing the Bathroom Floor

Sitting meditation is a gift I give myself. My logical mind says there is no time to meditate since there is so much work to be done. Cleaning is one of the things that I enjoy and every once in a while, in moments when I am absorbed in what I am doing, I have a glimpse of our interconnectedness with all that the eyes can see, all that there ever is, or was, our ignorance, the truth about suffering and the cause of suffering.

I have also come to one truth, that everything I have always wished for, prayed, has come true, which indicates that the material world is just a manifestation of what we think, what we envision. That something comes from pure thought is true.

I have now realized that there are several things I am obsessed about: Constant cleaning, indicative of the inherent disorder in my mind, constant worrying about money, an insecurity, constant fear of the future that prevents me from enjoying the present, the now, the only truth and the only reality. What I must do instead is to accept the present, enjoy it to the fullest because there is only now.

In this life, if we realize that our life is finite, in this body, and yet eternal, for the spirit, the soul, the light, the essence, IT (as Alan Watts calls it) always comes back until we have reached perfection in which case we no longer have to come back. Our existence in this lifetime is nothing but a school. The school of life, where every encounter is a lesson, every moment is a lesson, then magically, our worries diminish, our fears fade, not completely, but our anger, our greed, the game of one-upmanship is reduced to a lesson and when we suffer, we can accept the suffering and let it pass.

We look at the past and we say "Oh, so much energy wasted." It is wasted energy only to the extent that we regret. But what do we regret? Why do we regret? We think.

We believe that we could have done something else, but if only our judging minds will give up and realize that every moment is perfection in motion then there will be a space between the judging and the events and we will realize that we always did what we could do at the time.

Even this moment that I am scrubbing the bathroom floor and the phone is ringing off the hook.

I wish that in this moment, my son would appreciate our black lab more, walk her more, pet her more. While I expect it of him it is I who has not done any of that today. I have been so selfish ...I think only in terms of I, I, I, me, me, me. I am busy thinking of myself and how things affect me!

Oh, I am the one who should develop compassion... I pray with all of my heart that my heart be pure, that my mind be rid of all these clutter, that I am able to see things differently instead of being confined to this I that was created by my ego.

Everyday a Test

"Each man's life represents a road toward himself, an attempt at such a road, the intimation of a path. No man has ever been entirely and completely himself. Yet each one strives to become that -one in an awkward, the other in a more intelligent way, each as best as he can. Each man carries the vestiges of his birth, -the slime and eggshells of his primeval past-with him to the end of his days. Some never become human, remaining frog, lizard, ant.

Some are human above the waist, fish below. Each represents a gamble on the part of nature in the creation of the human. We all share the same origin, our mothers; all of us come in at the same door. But each of us -experiments of the depths- strives toward his own destiny, we can understand one another; but each of us is able to interpret himself to himself alone"-~Hermann Hesse, in "Demian."

Every day we are alive we experience a myriad of emotions. It is what reminds us of our humanity.
Anger is one of those fiery emotions, a colorful vista from the point of view of an ego which knows only the past. As long as we live we will at some point experience anger.

I suppose that every day of our lives is some kind of major test. How do we deal with anger, how do we deal with the inherent tendency to attack a perceived enemy. We observe it and then we let it go. We see the drama in our own minds but from the point of view of an audience, not a participant.

There is pain in having to attack an enemy, or a perceived enemy, for how can there be an enemy if there is only One? As I rummaged through the letters that I wrote, I found the draft of a letter to an old friend in graduate school who has hurt me deeply, I thought, and sought me ten years later.

Ten years is a long time and I knew that I have forgotten whatever was done then. Nonetheless I answered her letter.

Dear S,

Every meeting with another human being is an act of a covenant fulfilled. We only see the hurts as it pertains to our personalities and our stage of development at that time; it is not "us" who is experiencing the hurt. It is our egos, personalities, and our minds that interpret the actions of other human beings.

This "illusion" is brought about by our sense of duality, you, others, and me. But in truth there is no you, me, others, there is only One, born out of the breath of God. We are here, on this planet just to learn our lessons, the first and foremost being that we are all one, and one with Him who made us. Forgive me also, if my actions in the past has brought you pain in any way.

Until the point that we are enlightened we are bound by our karma and only when we realize that we are all in a path to finding God do we realize how senseless our actions have been, but we always begin anew. God will never abandon us. Take care. I will always be your friend, no matter what. We only forgot that momentarily, so now I am reminding you. Sincerely,

I no longer remember what the incident was, but there was a scar in my memory that I had to erase.

Our only enemy is our attachment to our perceived notions of ourselves. Perhaps in time we will get past our ignorance.

Smoke Gets In Our Eyes

It is 3 o'clock in the morning, the clock says. I start typing. I click the mail message button every 30 seconds. Did I get any e-mail? All of my friends are still asleep, or they are up and running and conquering the world, or their inner demons. Ah, but there are no demons, only inner dragons.

Our fears, our expectations, our entrapment in a body that grows old and dies. And then we repeat the cycle again and again and again.

I left the Philippines because I have always felt it too repressive. Now I know that that feeling of repression is really the soul searching to expand. I used to blame my parents for choosing the life that they did. Now I blame myself for not understanding as well as I do now and I console myself by saying that I was too young to understand. I was too young to understand.

I now know what it was. It is like the sannyasin going on a pilgrimage, except they did not cut their ties with us their children. I think they were too attached to us. It made their journey a little harder, but they got there.

I could give the book the title "Freedom is Not a Myth"-as opposed to that of Chogyam Trungpa's book, "The Myth of Freedom."

Freedom is not a myth, if one is willing to go to the depths of one's soul, experience the loneliest moments, and realize that God in His magnificence put us in this world, but the real purpose is so that we can find our way back to Him.

That never for a moment should we forget who we are and we are part of Him who gave us life, and all the pain and pleasure, hope and fear, loss and gain, fame and shame, praise and blame, the fulcrum that our personalities operate due to having forgotten who we really are, are but a way for us to remember who we were. Who we are. And the dance of life, no matter how fascinating is still a dance in illusion, for the entire world is illusion.

But it takes a lifetime to remove the shroud that covers our eyes.

Sometimes, it takes many, many lifetimes, repeated again and again, until our lesson is learned. We do learn it eventually.

I still have no idea what my function in life is, other than to view and be awed by the magnificence of God and His creations as well as appreciating the little miracles of everyday life. Like the weed that sprouts from the crack on the driveway and produces a magnificent yellow flower.

Our Relationships as Mirrors

Until we wake up, all of our relationships are karmic necessities and all of our actions proceed from birth to death. Our own reflex reactions are effects of a lifetime of conditioning until we choose not to buy into it anymore. Then we become conscious creators of our lives.

The world is a mirror of our thoughts. The beauty of being able to watch everything,including our thoughts bring empowerment for we know that we have the power to choose where the mind should land rather than the mind ruling everything. I look at everyone around me and I am reminded of my own self.

Our teachers are everywhere, but those that evoke the most intense feelings are those whose lives touch ours in more ways than a casual acquaintance.

In this moment my master teachers are the following:

One example is my friend the professor who is a perfect expression of the compassion and kindness that arises from a pure heart, without any thought attached to it. For his complete detachment from everything and everybody. He has the mind of a scientist, the soul of an artist (he plays the piano) and the heart of a sage.

Then there are my other friends who are climbing the corporate ladders as an expression of passion in me. The passion to make a difference.

My son and my dogs, who mirror the self absorption that I am so guilty of, selfishness, but also their pure innocence and also their ability to forget slights so easily. When my son was very young, I used to look at him and see complete helplessness, especially when he is asleep and it is so very interesting when sometimes he asserts himself so much it felt like he wanted to grow up too quickly.

And now he is no longer helpless. Perhaps I was the helpless one after all.

Like a Butterfly in a Garden Full of Flowers

Oh, this mind alights from one subject to another, there is no escaping, but why escape? Why not rather accept? This moment is as perfect as it should be, because God wills it. It is as it should be, perfect and complete.

We are drowned by so many voices in our heads; we fail to see that which is the One Voice. So many desires, wants, of physical comfort, of sensuality, of the appetites of all kinds all arising from the illusion of a solid physical body. All of the Masters have said this again and again and again. There is no solid entity.

I suppose that the best way to envision this is a plasma of some sort where we all are, and although there are some differences between the composition of the plasma and ourselves, enough for a form to emerge, there is enough similarity that this form is really merged with the plasma. I suppose that this only makes sense in my own mind.

Were I to draw a picture of anything, there will be no solid lines to separate the object from the surroundings. I would draw only a mere outline merging with the mist.

It is raining. I love the rain. I always think that it is God's way of communicating with us, raining his love upon us, so perfect, so forgiving and forgetting, so utterly all encompassing.

All we have to do is to remember that we deserve to be loved because God made us out of love for humanity, and there is nothing we can do to not merit that love. It is always a given, and it is vanity to think of ourselves as undeserving of love.

"Jesus wept". For even amongst the miracles he performed in the name of the Father, people still did not believe.

A kind and merciful God does not permit suffering and there is no paradox. Our sufferings are from our own minds. If we clear our minds, we will hear the symphony of the universe, and the voice of God. But how does one reach this? First have a clean and pure heart, and then obtain a serene and peaceful mind.

In two words, discipline and tenacity. There is no other way.

The Illusion of Time

The past is all blurry to me. I have to look at the records that I have in order to accurately remember things, events, milestones, births, deaths. Mostly I have forgotten most of the events that I am supposed to commemorate and so it is always a surprise when I look at my journal from several years past and am reminded of the pages that I tore, out of anger, frustration, desperation perhaps, or even then, the intense desire to erase memories.

There are very few things in my closet and drawers. There are very few things in the house really. I always say I can pack everything that I own in a car and take off but that is still a lot.

The wandering monks and the sannyasins carry only a blanket and a bowl in a box that they can use as a pillow and they carry this box on their backs. They have no past or future. Some of them have even left their families in search of themselves. They wander from place to place, live from the charity of others or from the trees in the forest. They have gone to a place where time does not exist.

In deep meditation, this is what we access. The place where no thought or time exists and we are simply being.

What is time? It is a measure of a process relative to the speed of light but if we are light then time has no meaning at all. Time is relative as evidenced by the fact that we accept what the clock says depending on where we live. Nine am in New York is six am in California. Still, as long as we live and perform our duties in this lifetime we will be reminded that our son has to be at the hairdressers at a certain time, that the lessons are at a certain time and that we need to take the dogs to the vet on a certain date.

We honor our engagements because they are necessary and we are always "on time" because we do not want to be the cause of someone else's anxiety, or our own. As long as we live in this lifetime we have to accept the illusion of time. It is our dharma in this life. Perhaps after several lifetimes we would be able to transcend both space and time.

For now, I have to get my son to his driving lesson.

The Many Loves of Our Lives

I read and admired Ayn Rand in my adolescent years. Perhaps it is the reason I have never really been "romantic". Nevertheless, I have experienced the desire to be "with someone". I thought it was expected, even necessary.

When I look back at the times in my life when I was in a romantic relationship, I see that those times were really a reflection of how I felt inside and the other person was only a mirror of that. To some this would sound callous and insensitive, to others it may make sense at some point, and still others who are willing to go within, it is true.

I heard this long before from a person who told me that marriage is only for the sake of the kids and for economic reasons. I thought it was cold at the time because I was young and foolish. Now I am old and still foolish but more aware of the simple truths in life. One of these is that each and every person that we are not casually associated with is a teacher in disguise, and just like school, we go from one lesson to the next until we graduate. Every association is a gift, a chance to get to know ourselves better.

I love. It is my wish to embody love and someday have a pure heart and find perfect peace. My son and my dogs are always a reminder to me of what pure love is. It was not always that way. They used to get jealous of each other for my time. I do not know if it is my perspective that has changed or the dogs and my son are older and therefore more accepting, or perhaps in an unwritten and silent way, they have come to know that I love them all equally. What does it matter? My heart gets full when my son brushes the dogs hairs, and when the dogs jump in joy when my son comes home from school.

I appreciate the simple pleasures in life.

Compassion and Detachment

Compassion is a key skill of a bodhisattva, but the bodhisattva's compassion comes from a place of true detachment. We can compare the actions of the enlightened ones to a person who is trying to save a drowning person.

Only the expert swimmers can do it and the first thing that they teach you as a lifeguard is that you have to hold the person by the neck and safely bring him to the shore because that person's first tendency is to cling to you and if you allow it, then there is a great possibility of both of you drowning.

If the one who is doing the rescue is on a boat, that person throws a raft but does not go with the raft. They throw the raft and it is tugged safely to the shore. These are special situations, but how do we deal with the everyday task of trying to be of help to someone who is a part of your life when they are in anguish over a loss, be it a loved one or a means of livelihood?

Compassion in a true sense does not entail sympathy or empathy. It is becoming solid like a rock, allowing the other person to sit on it until he or she decides to move on. No matter what we do or say which we think will make the other feel better can not compare to allowing the person to make decisions on their own. If a person is hungry, he or she has to make the decision to eat or not. After the decision is made, that person actually has to eat the food to alleviate hunger. The same is true of every emotion. It is so much easier for us to offer solutions as that is our first impulse.

When we do then we become part of that person's drama. We think that we are helping the other person when we do so and our egos become inflated with the thought that we helped someone but that is a conditioned reflex. Our egos want the "Thank you for helping me" part. It makes us happy because we "helped" another person.

We can not really help another human being, just as we can not really "teach" another person. We can show them the means to find their way but we can not really point to it. It is much harder to empower another human being that it is to offer food, money, advise of all sorts. When situations arise, we can simply listen and let be. No judgments necessary.

When You Look Into the Mirror

When we look into the mirror, what do we see? Why is it that sometimes the mirror says we are fat or thin, plain or pretty, dazzling or dull?

Mirrors reflect without feelings, water wets and then flows, always fluid. The perfect analogy of "detached from evil in the midst of evil and detached from good in the midst of good."

There are days when I do not see myself in the mirror. When I do, there is still an attachment to form that I sense in me. I judge my body, I judge my face, my hair, I judge the outfit that I am wearing. I still feel the need to be validated as this personality. Definitions after definitions.

The realized ones tell us time and time again that there is no abiding self, that each of us, are created moment to moment, and this wondrous body as ours is nothing but a shell that gets filled and emptied moment to moment.

As we cannot step on the same stream twice, so we cannot re-create who we were a moment ago, and to try to do so will only lead us into further delusion.. delusion after delusion.

To hang on to this solid self is heretical and also a means of "fooling ourselves and deceiving others" But how do we escape? As Chogyam Trungpa said in The Myth of Freedom "The absence of struggle is in itself freedom."

And I am still chasing sayings instead of letting be or simply being. I am trapped in words as I am trapped in the illusion of the solid self that I see when I face the mirror.

Perhaps when I am free, I can look into the mirror and see the light instead of the lines on my face or the graying hair on my head. Perhaps it is even possible in this lifetime.

To Forgive

I have always wondered why Gandhi never advocated a violent act against the British, or why the Dalai Lama is doing the same, and why Jesus asked His Father for forgiveness for all those that persecuted Him.

Real or perceived, there are injustices in the world. We are not able to fathom the depth and interconnectedness of events so we feel justified in feeling hurt and angry. We ask ourselves, why did my husband/wife/lover leave me? Why did my parents abuse me verbally/beat me physically/not love me enough? Why did my superior reprimand me in front of my other co-workers/give my promotion to someone else/fire me and on and on. Why did my parent/child/cousin/friend have to die just because a drunken driver lost control of his/her car?

Why did I lose my parent/child/friend in the war which I do not believe in in the first place? We cling to the memory of the past hurt because we feel justified in our anger, and we carry this anger and hurt to our next relationship. Sometimes we refuse to enter a new relationship because of all of these.

We make it our shield from further pain. Sometimes pain becomes our armor. Inside it we create the illusion of being invulnerable. Other times we make it our prison when we can choose to walk out. We don't walk out because we hang on to our sense of justice, our sense of being justified in our feelings.

Somehow it is more comfortable to be there, imprisoned by our thoughts, imprisoned by the past.

Sometimes we want to exact revenge, in any way or manner that we think will hurt the other person who we think hurt us. We can use the rationalization that we are only humans and we are not gods, but Jesus in his humanity is a reminder of us of the love of God. Perhaps we could turn it around and say Jesus as the Son of God could have chosen to punish.

All of us have suffered some pain in one way or another. All of us at some point has condemned another and wished we could take revenge. That is in the past. Imagine how the world will be when there is no anger anymore. We can choose to relive the past right now. Every moment that we spend in reminiscing the hurt of the past is taking away from the enjoyment of the present. Why choose to suffer?

Jesus never condemned and therefore has no need to forgive. In His humanity Jesus wept when Lazarus died, not because his friend died but because of the imperfection of the faith of the people who saw Him part the sea, heal the afflicted and even raise the dead. To forgive, we must first condemn, but how can we condemn when we do not know completely?

We see only a fraction of reality through the lenses that we put on.

Jesus has no karma, and in my mind, Gandhi and the Dalai Lama fully know the meaning of what the scriptures from a thousand years say "To take offense is the same as to offend" for with every act or event or person that we condemn, we enter the cycle of rebirth, once more. No one is immune to this. If we feel the pain, if we acknowledge it and then we let it go then perhaps there is a chance for us to see through the illusion. Perhaps then we would realize what Jesus meant when he said "The kingdom of heaven is within."

Anger as a Conditioned Response

The people capable of inciting our deepest emotions are the ones that we are in deep relationships with in this lifetime. Our families, our lovers,our friends and those whom we work with have lessons to teach us. The source of anger is always a fear for an imagined loss.

I missed the exit to the DMV when I took my son to take his driver's permit. He was upset as this would delay his coming back home. There were a couple of times I hesitated to go ahead of another driver at the intersection and he got more upset. I can feel myself feeling the annoyance, first at myself, and then at him for telling me what to do. I had to turn around but that was not an easy task either and there was a time when I felt myself getting really angry that I had to stop. I can feel the blood rising to my face and I can feel the constriction on my throat. This is what happens when I feel angry. Rewind.

I got angry because he knew the way better than I did. My anger was a reaction to the perceived loss of respect and my mind projected it to loss of love. I got angry because I am taking a valuable day off so that I can take him. I got angry because I have to do everything myself, and my mind goes on and on and on, spinning the threads like a cocoon, but unwisely and frantically spinning around me, thus cutting off air, the breath of life. The drama continues. I assumed that a passport is good enough as an identification. We had to go back home and get his birth certificate.

Erase and recapture. It was my own mind that was creating all of this chaos. There is no one else and there is nothing else outside of me that created the anger, the throat constriction. I go back to my childhood when we did what our parents told us without question.

To answer a parent would have been such an irreverent act, it becomes a source of shame. No one did it. It was my own conditioning which I expected of my son to repeat.

Rerun. We come home with his permit and he was very proud and happy and I realized how funny it is now that I missed the exit because I had to take that exit every week to take him to his ice hockey lessons a few years back. How can I forget? I did.

Movie over. Life begins anew.

Anchoring as a Tool

Anchoring is the process of putting a thought together with certain action and then linking the two together so that when the action is performed, the thought comes to mind. We can use anchoring as a tool for meditation or as a tool for manifestation. Anchoring in case becomes a tool for us to be grounded in our being.

To those who are seeking liberation anchoring is another way to get into meditation.

The ancients have taught us that meditation is the way out of suffering, but formal sitting meditation is only one way.

We can do meditation while we are in action.

I can give examples and the one that always comes to mind is when the Buddha talked to a grandmother who told him that she too wishes to be enlightened, however, she does not have the time to sit down and meditate since she is responsible for too many people. I compare her to the CEO of a corporation or the Principal Investigator in a research laboratory, or a mother who has to take care of her children, earn a living, keep house, take care of aging parents, attend to other siblings and so on and so on.

Our responsibilities will always be there, especially knowing that we are the writer, director and producer of our lives. We choose the roles that we play and we choose to create the movies of our lives.

When we have chosen these roles, there is still a means to anchor ourselves, to be grounded in our being. For example, as we take showers, we can say "As I cleanse this body, may I also cleanse my mind", "As I brush my teeth, may I also brush the dust off my mind", "As I scrub this floor, may I also clean my thoughts". One can create any anchor that they wish.

Anchoring is also a means to remind us of the power of thought to manifest our desires, whatever it is that we desire.

With the use of anchoring, it is possible to bring other desires to reality. As a coach, I am not allowed to tell my clients what to do, as I have not the right to take away their power to choose their course of action. However, I teach them how to use anchoring in my sessions, as a means to manifest their desires whatever it is that they desire. I do not ask them what they desire and we have full understanding that whatever they desire will come to them at the right time and under the right circumstances if and only if it is good for them and that what they desire can not harm another being.

When one wishes to apply anchoring to material creation, then one can use it to remind himself or herself that material thing he or she wishes to manifest. For example as one drinks tea in the morning, one can say "I, (your name) now have (the object that one desires)and then get into the feeling of having what it is that one desires. The key is to be present in the here and now.

Either way, we use anchoring to bring us back to the core of our being, no matter what it is that we are doing.

Taming Our Inner Dragons

The three headed dragons that inhabit our minds are fear, doubt and worry.

There are many faces of fear, but the most prevalent in all of us is the fear of getting old and dying. When I was ten years old and I was looking at my aunt who was then forty, I thought to myself I will never look like that. I can not use my mother as my gauge since she had always watched herself and even at 68 when she passed on, she looked as young as I thought of her when I was in high school. Now, when I see myself in the mirror, there is only a glimmer of what I used to see when I was young. There are many lines which I never noticed before.

In my home in Connecticut, after a long sitting meditation I have faced the vision death as I was falling asleep. I asked the cloaked vision if it had come to get me, and it said "not yet, however, I want you to know that I exist". What that encounter taught me was that we never know when our time is, so we do the best we can before our time. It is easier for me to accept that fact since in our household, when I was growing up, we were always taught that there is freedom from suffering after the body dies.

Our doubt arises from a sense of unworthiness. I have to keep reminding everyone, even myself once in a while, that we are already worthy when we were born. To be alive is such a gift, but it is also a given so we forget and take it for granted. Now I do things with complete assurance that whatever will be, will be. I know from experience that my physical actions have very little to do with the outcome.

It is the intent that matters the most, and the intent has to come from a place of peace, of faith. We doubt because we think that what we want is not possible for us because we are not worthy.

Worry is of the future. We anticipate and we project. Usually we project the worst that could happen and that would be fine if we are able to transcend these thoughts, but more often than not, it results in our inability to sleep or even take action in the present moment. We worry about how things might turn out, the thoughts paralyze us and consequently results in our inability to be simply present where we are. I know now that the present is much more fun! As I get older I am able to laugh at myself more often. I realize now that my past worries robbed me of sleep and peace of mind and the time I could have been enjoying with my loved ones.

Every once in a while our inner dragons will try to rise and try to assert their presence. We simply have to remember that we put them there ourselves and we can befriend them until we come to a point that can remove them at will. Until that time, we tame them, one dragon at a time.

Right Action - Effective Action

In the beginning of my spiritual journey many years ago, I wondered why Jesus turned the tables of the money changers in the temple instead of simply asking them to leave. I was used to thinking of compassion as gentle, loving and kind.

Overturning the tables was bold, some might even think it rash. That was then. Now, there is no doubt in my mind that what Jesus did was the right action. He did not have to think. It was immediate. Such an action was skillful compassion. It was the means, at the time, that he used to make them aware of their actions. A means to awaken them.

How do we know what right action is? The rules are written, and they are rules written in different ways in different religions. Among these are the maxims we were taught as children. We should not lie, cheat or steal. We must not kill. Is it a sin to lie if telling the truth would mean giving someone away for them to get killed? Is it wrong to steal food? Will it be wrong for a mother to defend herself and her children from someone who seeks their life? Was it sacrilegious of David to eat the food reserved for the priests while he was in hiding?

It is said that the Buddha offered himself to a hungry mother lion which had been trapped in a thicket and was too weak to get out and hunt for food. The Buddha felt compassion for the mother lion and the two cubs. In the story it was also written that the Buddha had a glimpse of the future and knew that giving himself up to be food also meant he is hastening his own evolution. This action is still bound by karma since he knew that sacrificing himself would still initiate another round of rebirth.

In the Bhagavad Gita, Arjuna was tormented with the thought of having to battle his own kin, and in the beginning refused to fight. In his agony, he questions God whether what he feels is real compassion or only a delusion. He was bound by sorrow since going to war meant he has to slay his own kinsmen to win the battle, until Krishna in the form of Govinda, his charioteer came to him.

The entirety of the Bhagavad Gita is Arjuna's realization that we are in this world and that life is not unlike a play. We have roles to play and we do them without attachment to the outcome. We make each act an offering to God.

While the written laws appear to be absolute, we see time and time again that these rules are applied differently each time. It all boils down to attachment. When we see the truth in what we are doing then the laws are at best guidelines. We see that right and wrong are only dictated by the circumstances. A person who is aware does right action all the time and does efficient action all the time. He is free from the judgment of his action, or the action of any man, as right or wrong.

I remember reading a great story about Gandhi. I do not recall clearly what it was. It involved a lot of people ready to march against the British as a form of protest. At the moment when many people were gathered, many having come from different places in support of his cause, Gandhi decided to cancel the protest march. His advisers told him that too many people were involved and that they had come from too many places and they are ready to go.

The advisers told Gandhi that they would lose ground in their crusade if he canceled the march, and he answered simply "My only commitment is to truth." This is a beautiful example of detached action.

In this lifetime, we have to play many roles, we have to wear many hats. We perform these roles the best that we know how and until we realize the answer to the question "Who Am I?" we are caught in the cycle of birth and death once more.

If we offer every act to God, then every action becomes skillful action and is therefore devoid of the accompanying karma. We must do our duty without attachment to the outcome and perhaps, even by our every day actions we might find God.

We Only Have Moments

I grew up in a small village which did not have televisions at the time I was growing up. I heard radio dramas when I was a little kid which brought my auditory senses far more developed in terms of recording and remembering than when I simply read materials. Perhaps it is the reason why I get very tired when I watch television, but I do remember the songs in the commercials. I am an auditory learner and I used to delight in listening to the commercials on television when I actually have my eyes closed for resting in between the scenes.

I remember very well the old commercial used to run by Kodak "Celebrate the moments of your life." I remember the song very well but could not really remember what the ad is about. Something about a camera capturing the moments in our lives. The camera is an instrument of precision which tries to capture moments at a certain angle, but it is impossible to capture the moment all at once. We use the photographs to remind ourselves of those moments that evoked feelings. Mostly we try to remember the happy moments. But the camera is an impersonal tool. The photographs only mean something to those of us who were present in an event and even then, they may, we may forget completely.

Children always live in the moment. They have no memory of the past and no concern for the future and are therefore, free.
As we get older we imbibe the imprints of our parents, our peers, and even our enemies. We get locked up in the definition of

ourselves that we unconsciously created. Still there are times when we are older that we are living life the way children do, and then we have no memory of what happened.

When we are in the moment, there is nothing to remember. We were the moment and we moved on. We may even get surprised at the photographs we are looking at and ask, I was there, was I not? There are really no big celebrations in life. The truth is that we only have moments, and the film only tries to capture that tiny moment in time. I suppose we take pictures to show our children and grandchildren what we did a long time ago, or we take pictures to remind us what we did a long time ago.

Where did the time go?

We are so used to thinking in terms of tomorrow, we forget about the NOW. Now is when we decide to pursue our dreams or have the excuse of getting stuck in the thought of "When................., then I will ...."

When we look at the old photographs, we realize that life is not a rehearsal. That was it. This is it. We only live one moment at a time. It is this moment when we have the power to choose. We choose to have peace moment by moment, we choose to be happy, moment by moment, we choose to enjoy the sunset and take our eyes off of the computer for a few minutes to marvel at God's creations, and we choose to be aware of our Self-the breath of God within-one breath at a time.

The Seven D's of Manifesting Our Innermost Desires

There are seven steps for manifestation, each of which is essential in the process. In order to fully appreciate the process of manifesting, you will need a stack of blank papers and a pen or a pencil to do the exercises. Print the article and do the exercises for each step, one paper per step.

1. Deep gratitude

Of the seven steps in manifesting, deep gratitude is the most important, for in the feeling of being grateful for the present, what is right here and right now, we communicate to God that we are right where He wants us to be and we are grateful for the gift of life.

When we feel grateful for what we have, we are communicating to the source of all. The feeling of sincere gratitude connects us to the source. Your task, write at least seven things that you are grateful for. Eventually, you can work it up, but day after day, you must write something to be grateful for. Pay attention to your feelings as you write them down.
Unless you have done and mastered this step, and you sincerely feel grateful in your heart, do not proceed to the next step.

2. Desire

The desire to change, whether physically, mentally, emotionally, financially or spiritually is a human emotion. It is our impetus to evolve. As humans, living on this planet in this lifetime, we will always feel some kind of desire. Even the desire to be desireless is desire. We acknowledge it, we accept it and we honor it.

Within every desire is the seed for achieving that desire but behind every desire is souls' yearning to experience life and to expand. Whether we realize it or not, all of our efforts will ultimately lead us to God. It may take many lifetimes, but union with God is our ultimate goal. We are on this journey and no matter how long it takes, as long as we learn our lessons lifetime after lifetime, we will get there.

Desire is not the same as yearning, for God wants us to have what we want for ourselves if He deems it will be good for us in the long run. Your task is to write seven desires every day. Be excited about each of your desires.

3. Decision

We honor our desires knowing that it was put there as a seed for growth and achievement, and that such a desire, when we feel it, is necessary for our evolution as a human being. We decide that the desire is a cue to change but we also acknowledge the fact that we have to initiate change from within. We decide that we are willing to make a change from the inside. We decide to let go of everything that is not in alignment with our goals.

We might experience pain in this process but deep within we know that it is for our own good. If we have to grow beyond our current circumstance we have to leave things and people behind.

Perhaps we will meet them again in the future, but it will be under different circumstances. We let go of the habits, thought patterns, outmoded ideas and even people when we decide that we have to move on. Your task is to write "I decide" seven times. Assume a feeling of already having what you desire. Ultimately, you know what is good for you and what is not so it is okay for you to change/erase any of the desires in your list.

4. Direction or Divine guidance

God, the source of all there is, communicates to us through our hearts. Our hearts never lie. Our minds can fool us into logical routes but the heart that speaks the truth and it is our hearts that is our conduit to God. Listen to your heart in every act. In this step, we align our thoughts, feelings and actions with what is true for us.

The fact is that we can only be of help to others when we have already worked on ourselves and this take. Your task is to write down seven possible avenues for obtaining you desire. A repeat of number 1, except that now, in the silence you are listening to your inner Self, the one that is always connected to God.

5. Determination

We are determined to pursue our goals and we do not let anyone or anything, including our own old thought patterns, distract us from our goal, and most importantly we enjoy the pursuit of our goals in the process.

We do not let well meaning people to dissuade us from going after our dreams because we know that even if they have our best interests at heart, their perspectives are limited by their own experiences. It is their own experience, their own dramas that they are basing their advice from and we do not have to live in it. We can create our own.

Your task is to write down at least seven reasons why what you desire is good for you. Focus on how good it feels to have what you desire.

6. Due diligence

We honor the natural laws of the universe in the pursuit of our goals. We plant the seed, we water it and then we tend to it day after day. While we can make the plant grow faster with music and with talking to it, the seed to form that plant sprouts in perfect accordance with its genetic makeup. We do day by day what needs to get done and we do our best, knowing that what we decide to do requires our best foot forward, day after day.

Your task is to write down seven things that you can do every day that will lead you closer to your goals and to follow those tasks to completion. At the end of the day, you will have a list of the things you accomplished, you feel successful and success builds on success. Create your day by thinking that you are on your way toward the fulfillment of your desire and the tasks that you wrote are necessary but you are doing them happily, enthusiastically.

At the end of the day go back to the reasons why it is good for you to have what you desire. Feel grateful for having it, even if you don't see it yet.

7. Detachment

Of the seven Ds this is the most trying and probably the hardest to follow. We are used to thinking in a linear time scale, and depending on our conditioning we think that our goals are not being met because we do not see any evidence of it immediately in our limited sight. This is where absolute faith is necessary, and it requires perfect surrender. We surrender our will to a higher being because God sees the bigger vision of things and we have to accept that whatever we wish for will be granted if and only if it is good for us in the grander design of our lives.

We accept that what we desire will be ours at the perfect time and under perfect circumstances.

Your task is to write down "Your will is my will. Thy will be done" seven times.

Repeat the process for each desire that you have. Keep the papers out of the sight of anyone but yourself for now. Later on, you can teach others how to do it. In the beginning it is your duty to cultivate faith.

Happy Manifesting!

May you always be blessed with everything your heart desires and remember that we can always have access to the infinite wisdom and unbounded love that is God.

We simply have to reach out in silence and in deep gratitude and we have to consider ourselves worthy of it.

Choosing to Stop the Karmic Wheel From Turning

Most of the artwork that I was exposed to and still remember was from a class in college where we had to analyze paintings after paintings. In my English classes, we read and analyzed books after books, written by the great minds.

Classical music I have loved since I was little, not knowing who the composers were or what the titles were until much later.

The mind is to me the most fascinating attribute of human beings. From it came the great works: Van Gogh's paintings, Mozart's concertos, Rodin's sculptures, Da Vinci's contributions in many fields, the contributions in science of Richard Feynman and Albert Einstein, and, the magnificent films that I am so very fond of. Yes, I consider films as a great art form, as I do prose and poetry. We enjoy the contributions of great minds with a desire for expression. And yet from the minds of men can also emerge the most heinous of crimes. What has history taught us?

The mind can be a tool for creation as well as a means to device destruction. Every action is rooted in desire and every desire is rooted in karma.

Desire is a very basic human emotion, whether it is a desire for power or for recognition or for money. The question remains. Why? Every thought, every action has a karmic origin. Each and every one of us is here to fulfill a unique purpose. It is up to us to find out what that purpose is and then perhaps we will understand our situations in life much better. Perhaps we can understand why there appears to be such disparity between nations and between individuals, why some people were born to become heads of states and others to die of starvation, why others were born to serve and others to be served.

The television in my home is approaching 34 years, as are the stove and the refrigerator. They all work fine, and maybe someday I will have to buy new ones but for now, they are perfect for my needs. We do not subscribe to cable television for the very reason that I really like to watch television.

In my friend's home is a very big screen television and I am allowed to flip the channels as much as I like when I visit. There appears to be 200 some channels that are available to watch. One channel that I stayed longer had the royal tots..sons and daughters of the rich and famous and their toys. The show flashed miniature Jaguars and Ferraris and real ponies as their toys as well as lavish parties for the birthdays. That was interesting, but what was more interesting was that presently, the Sultan of Brunei has a royal palace that can fit several White Houses!

A few years back, the Sultan of Brunei was reportedly the richest man in the world. Reportedly he had $40 billion dollars. At that time, Bill Gates reportedly had $6.7 billion. Things change as everything does. Empires rise and fall. Country leaders change, fame fades away, fortunes change hands.

The fame and fortune that one has in this lifetime is already a product of previous life work.

Call it the karmic bank where one can deposit and withdraw at any one time. The only difference between this karmic bank and a regular bank is that we share ours with all others in our lifetime.

The Sultan of Brunei, as we all did, chose to be born in this lifetime to fulfill a unique role. The Sultan has great privilege and with it comes great responsibility.

When the Buddha was born, the wise men in his father's palace predicted that he would either be a great king or a great sage. What made him renounce his kingdom, his beloved family and every form of attachment? He chose to stop the wheel of karma from turning, but that choice was made in one lifetime after having gone through many lifetimes. There is only one thing for sure, and that is his choice was moment to moment until he realized enlightenment.

We can not know where we are in this turning wheel but we too can choose, moment to moment, what to think, how to act and what to do. By our thoughts and actions we are either making a deposit to our karmic bank or we are making a withdrawal. When we choose to sit and meditate, while watching our breath, we are at that moment choosing to stop the turning of the karmic wheel. When we get up we again turn the wheel. So the world turns and we perform our chosen tasks in this lifetime, knowing that each breath is our connection to the past and the future, and that each breath is also what equalizes us with the billion dollar minds as well as the homeless.

Every road leads to God and we might get distracted by the toys and the toils of this lifetime but we all get back on track eventually. How long we choose to get there is our greatest gift.

The Fruits of Our Attachments

My library at home has multiple copies of the same books. I buy the same titles when I see them at garage sales and at Goodwill. I hope to give them someday to someone who will ask for them. I watch the same films over and over in an old VCR and I use my son's PlayStation to watch the DVDs. I learn something about myself from each viewing. Life is the same way. Until we learn all of the lessons in this lifetime, we will come back and be a part of the same movie again and again. Different faces will play the characters but the movie will be a remake of the previous one. We have to learn from this lifetime and we have to do it alone. There is no one who could do it for us.

I had a pretty nondescript childhood. My parents were deeply religious and it was a ritual in the village to go to church on Saturdays. That was our Sabbath. My father was a minister and he lectured after the mass and afterwards we would go to other people's homes or they would come to ours and discuss about the village life and God.

My mother's parents owned the greater portion of the village but they lived in town a few miles away. Part of the land was taken care of by a caretaker and the other portions they sublet to other farmers in the village and then just collected money at harvest season when the crops have been sold. We farmed what was not sublet to other farmers.

For crops we had rice, sugarcane, coconuts, mandarin oranges and lots and lots of other fruits and vegetables. We had cattle, pigs, chickens and ducks for meat. We managed the rice mill and the coconut mill that my grandfather owned. It was idyllic. I played with handmade toys: balls we made from straws and dolls made by my eldest sister. I played softball with other kids but I enjoyed playing in the rain best. My mother who was going to be a medical doctor and became a teacher instead stopped teaching after having five children. Mostly she prayed all day. We had people taking care of the laundry and my older sisters did the cooking. Life was peaceful.

My aunts and uncles who lived in the town where my grandparents lived ran businesses. They had very large homes with swimming pools. They owned multiple vehicles and had maids, drivers and the equivalent of butlers. The only thing I remember them doing was being constantly on the telephone and giving parties almost every weekend. My cousins had music lessons, dance lessons and tutors. They wore hand tailored clothes made of imported fabric.

I don't remember when my grandfather decided to take away control of the land from my parents. I must have been very young. I began to feel the first pangs of suffering. My oldest sister had to work in the city bakery to help the family. When my sister brought me a present-a pink dress from the city as a Christmas present- and I told her I didn't like it, so take it back because I wanted lace, it was the first time I saw my father really angry. He ordered me to take it and thank my sister or else. I refused. He beat me with a leather belt until my mother stopped him.

I learned how to be grateful. Looking back, even as a child I had memories of wearing real lace from a long time back. It could not have been from this lifetime.

Like Adam and Eve eating from the tree of knowledge and discovering themselves naked, I learned some truths about life. I was eight years old. I began to question my parent's decision to marry each other. Mostly, I blamed my mother for marrying my father. In the Philippines, men are allowed to marry down, not women. An unwritten yet very real economic caste system was in place, a remnant of the Spanish occupation for four hundred years. I know now that my father felt both shame and sadness for not having the money to buy what I wanted himself. Or perhaps he was sad that I could not understand that we did not have the money to buy real lace.

I saw the pain in my father's eyes that lasted for decades until he passed away. He dealt with dignity what was handed to him and made the best that he could. We no longer had help and had to do most of the chores ourselves. When I was born, they thought I was going to be a boy and when I turned out to be a girl he treated me like a boy anyway. I spent most of my time with him until.

I went away to my grandparent's home at twelve years old to go to high school. I loved the time I spent with him while he tilled whatever land my grandfather gave us, this time all by himself. We hauled drinking water from an artesian well a half mile away with pushcarts. Even then, I knew that wisdom did not come from education. While my mother taught me how to read and write at five, my father told me stories in the bible and what they meant.

From my father I learned unconditional love. From my mother I learned the freedom to choose, the freedom from the dictates of society and the discipline of detachment. That was my lesson from them in this lifetime.

My parents both passed away a very long time ago. I blamed myself for having been hard on them. I am now the parent. I wonder if my son would judge me harshly too?

I hope that when I pass on, I would have relinquished all desire to come back. I hope to learn everything that I can in this lifetime so that when the moment comes, I will no longer have the attachments of this lifetime and I can remain where I came from. I wish to be awakened from the dream of this lifetime and remain with my creator.

No Traces Left

This story has been mentioned in many Zen books.

Two monks, one who was just starting his study and one who has been a monk for a long time were on a trip to study with another Zen master. While traveling came upon a woman who wanted to cross the river but did not want her clothes to get wet. As purity of mind and body was an important lesson, the old monk refused. The young monk on the other hand merrily carried the woman on his shoulders across the river, and afterwards, they went on their way and she went her way.

A long time has passed and the old monk finally spoke, reprimanding the young monk.

"I can not believe you carried her across the river. We are not supposed to have bodily contact with a woman!", the old monk said to the young one in a self-righteous tone. The young monk answered "Friend, I carriedxpndtw-8 her across the river several hours ago and then I put her down. You are still carrying her on your shoulders."

When I look around my house and see clutter, I am reminded of my friend who owns a house that is four times as big. She keeps it almost always, immaculate. She hires no one to clean it for her. Very simply, she puts everything away as she is done with them. When she cooks, as soon as the meal preparation is complete, the kitchen would be spotless, as if no activity had occurred there and the sumptuous meal just magically appeared on the table. She does all action completely, no traces left. This is how she does everything in her daily life, always, completely in the moment.

Our minds are so filled with desires, unfinished projects, reminders of what to do tomorrow and plans for the future we tend to do multitasking. It is not possible to do two things simultaneously and be fully present. We delude ourselves into thinking that we can multitask but if we simply look inward honestly, we will see that what we have is unfinished tasks, unfinished business, piled on top of one another.

To cultivate moment to moment awareness, to finish something completely, requires one pointed focus on the task at hand. It is as if we were burning a log and when it is burnt completely, only the ashes are left. It is true whether we are folding clothes or washing dishes, or negotiating a complicated business deal, or planning a trip to an exotic place, or creating multimillion-dollar projects. We do not look back and judge, did we do it well?"

The next moment is a new moment. Another task begins and we see the completion of it. When we can cultivate this moment to moment awareness, we feel peaceful, we see the space around which all of the events are happening of which we are only a part of. Once in a while, we get a glimpse of freedom.

The Universality of Suffering

When Prince Gautama, whose father shielded him from the realities of life outside the palace stepped out, he learned the first noble truth, the truth of sickness, old age, and death. The truth of suffering. It is a privilege to live as a human being, but privilege always comes with responsibility. Until we realize enlightenment in this lifetime there will always be something that will cause us to suffer. How do we deal with it?

I read this story a long time ago and could not remember the book from which to quote it.

Once a distraught widow came to the Buddha. Her young son was playing in the yard and was bitten by a snake. He died. The woman cried "It must have been a terrible mistake, please, please revive him". The Buddha told her "First bring me a seed from a household which has not experienced any suffering." The woman went and knocked on every door on the village and told them of her plight.

She was searching for a seed. When sunset came, the woman came back to the Buddha, weary and beaten.

"Have you brought me a seed?"he asked the woman. "No, enlightened one. There is no household in our village which has not suffered any pain." "You have learned the first Noble truth. Go and bury your son."

This story illustrates that suffering comes with life. If we came into this world as a consequence of our karma, we are bound to experience some kind of suffering, be it mental or physical suffering, for we would not have relinquished the preferences of the previous lifetimes, the memory of the forgotten past hidden from view.

Our attachments bind us. Our desires arise and as one desire is fulfilled, another one arises. We fear not getting what we desire and that causes us to suffer. We feel attached to people, our beliefs and material things. We are attached to our pets. We are attached to our identities in his lifetime.

God does not want us to suffer. He is not a punitive God. The cause of our suffering is our forgetfulness of our true nature, that we always have been and always will be part of Him. This is the only thing we have to remember. His laws are universal and impartial. When we feel that we are suffering due to an illness, a lost promotion, not having what we desire, then it is because we have forgotten this connection in pursuit of our own ego based desires. We feel mental pain in the form of being frustrated, angry or sad, and being in this body, we feel bodily pain.

There is a way out of suffering. The first is by deep and absolute surrender to the higher power, to God, and the second is by meditation which will allow us to accept the emotion fully, whether it is anger or grief or frustration or physical pain, and then releasing it, completely.

This does not mean that we are going to act out our anger. It means accepting the fact that in this moment, we are angry but we do not have to lash back at the person or event that precipitated the anger. If we grieve, we grieve fully in the best way we know how. Some grieve by bawling, some by being silent, some by keeping away from other people. There is a proviso that one must not harm oneself or others when fully experiencing grief.

To deal with frustration one must acknowledge the fact that frustration is clinging to a perceived loss, and behind that still is the feeling that there is nothing else one can do. It is a feeling of helplessness. We attribute it to an event not completely controlled by us, hence we feel frustrated. We have to bring ourselves to the realization that at the moment that we did what was done, we did the best that we could, therefore there is no need to blame ourselves or others. We can not undo what has already been done so we accept it's consequences. Wallowing in self pity or blaming others will only plummet us into a cycle of dis-empowerment .

Physical pain comes with having a physical body and we deal with it not as an inconvenience, not as having to fight with. We simply accept that this is what we have in this lifetime and we deal with what happens, accordingly. We get born into a body, the body gets old and eventually dies. Only that which animates the body is immortal. We chose the body we are in long before we were born. We chose who our parents will be, our siblings and everyone around us to maximize learning in this lifetime. It is not easy to comprehend this at the intellectual level but it is the truth.

Where we are right now is an effect of where we were many lifetimes ago. The only way we can skip this is when we are able to choose at will when and where to be reborn, if we choose to, and that can only be a consequence of awakening in this lifetime. Until then, our rebirth is a consequence of our past.

No matter what our current circumstances in life, as long as we live there will be some kind of perceived suffering. It comes with the territory of being alive as a human being. It unites us all, just as the breath does. We need to be reminded of our true Self,then perhaps we could deal with the pain better.

Chogyam Trungpa wrote this story in one of his many books:

When the great sage Milarepa's son died, he wept. One of his disciples asked him "Teacher, did you not teach us that everything is illusion?". He answered "Yes, but this is super illusion."

Even those who have already worked on themselves constantly still have vestiges of humanly suffering.

We can only deal with where we are, right now. We can choose to prolong the suffering by fighting it or we can choose to alleviate it, if not end it, by simply accepting the moment as it is and refusing to cling to the past. The present moment is always new. In the present moment there is freedom and with freedom comes power.

Acquiring Intuitive Knowledge by Disciplining the Mind

One who has conquered others is powerful, but one who has mastered himself is mightier still-Lao Tzu

The Buddha sat in meditation after awakening to the true nature of his being. Jesus Christ went and prayed for 40 days by Himself in the mountains before he came back to his disciples. When there was nothing else to attain, why did they do it?

It is said that one of the tests that the Tibetan monks had to go through during their training is to dry a wet blanket draped over them by generating the heat from their body while sitting on top of a snow- covered mountain. If he failed, he had to do it again and again and again until he passed. This is a test of the human spirit, a test of wills, a matter of discipline.

We normally think of discipline in the harsh sense: having to do something that is not natural to us, and yet there is another sense of discipline that we tend to overlook. That which comes natural to us we no longer regard as discipline, and yet it is. Our task is simply to remember who we are: spiritual beings having a human experience, then everything comes naturally. We don' t have to think of "disciplining" ourselves.

We do not have to think of always being honest, we do not have to think that we eat to nourish our bodies, we do not have to think of going to bed on time in order to wake up early the next day to do what we have to do, and we do not have to think of doing what we have to do. We simply do them with our whole body and mind, in the present moment. Then there is nothing to regret, nothing to strive for, nowhere to hurry.

It is impossible to do wrong when we are aware of ourselves in the present moment, for in this present moment is perfection, as it is the next moment.

We simply have to be here. If there is any discipline required, it is and can only be, to be fully present.

The Japanese tea ceremony is a very formal ritual and yet every movement of the person who is serving tea is an embodiment of harmony. This is the essence of Zen, action without the rigidness of thought. This is what being with the flow, being in Tao, means. Chaos only occurs when we are doing something and yet we are elsewhere in thought.

We live in such a fast paced society we hardly ever experience anything as they are, and then we complain. We complain to our friends, to our spouses, to our children or to anyone else who would listen. We complain to God. We have no time to listen to the silence and yet it is in silence where we find all the answers. It is possible for us to develop intuitive knowledge if we simply listen to silence.

Intuitive knowledge is knowledge beyond intellectual reasoning. We all have it. The problem is that we are too busy doing instead of being. We pray (usually) telling God everything we desire, in a one way conversation. How do we know that our prayers are answered when we do not really listen? In the silence of our thoughts lies the answer to every question that we have, the solution to our every perceived problem.

It is in disciplining our minds that we acquire intuitive knowledge and when we have realized it we see that everything that we do, everything that we are, is flow, from one moment to the next, in a seamless sequence.

The outcome of discipline is freedom. Without it, we will forever feel trapped. Perhaps we can re-define freedom as the absence of resistance, the acceptance of each moment as it is.

Waiting For Enlightenment

My son went on another extended trip this time to a debate camp 2000 miles away from home and I am theoretically on vacation. Vacation from what? Before he left we had a spat because he always waits till the last minute to pack. I was particularly mad because I have ten thousand things to do and his flight was at 6 o'clock in the morning the following day.

When I came home from the airport and took a look at the house I almost cried because there was no space in the house that was not cluttered with paper. And then it hit me. All the clutter was mine! The chairs and the tables were all filled with paper. Everywhere there was paper. His room was, though not meticulously clean, uncluttered, just like his mind. I could not even blame the dogs for the clutter. True, there was hair everywhere from our maturing black labrador, but all of the paperwork was mine!

It finally dawned on me. It seems that I am always waiting for something which I can never really define. I am always so caught up in the mini-dramas of everyday life that I had failed to notice many things around me.

Today I ran out of excuses. My dogs were not cluttering the house. My son's clutter is confined to the burlap carpet in his room and if one opens his drawers they are meticulously in order, with the exception of his clothes drawers.

There are some people that do not have to go through the same arduous paths towards realization. They are spontaneously enlightened and do not have to be affected by the projected matrix of suffering that the Buddha spoke of. They come to this world and see it just as it is, nothing more than a playground. So they play and act their respective roles and go on, but unaffected and as mentioned by Thomas Cleary in Minding Mind, those are the people that have already gone through the evolutionary process many lifetimes over and only come back to help others in the path. So they live and they play never forgetting that their role is to help others get out of the bondage of suffering.

They do not have to go through hours of sitting in meditation anymore. They are compassionate and detached, kind and naturally forgiving, and although clothed in the personality of this shared reality's birth, they never once forget who they are. Bodhisattvas. They always know that enlightenment is exactly where one is, and all one has to do is see. No more seeking, just seeing and being.

The Perfect Sage of Chogyam Trungpa

"Just as the sun dispels darkness, the perfect sage has conquered the false habits of mind. He does not see the mind or the thoughts derived from the mind" - From "Cutting Through Spiritual Materialism" by Chogyam Trungpa

I have read this book at least a dozen times-not all of it-but parts of it, over and over. Every time I read it, a new insight begins and a new question arises.

Then he quotes from "The Heart Sutra", the Tibetan Version:

"The Mantra of transcendent knowledge, the mantra of deep insight, the unequalled mantra, the mantra that calms all suffering, should be known as truth, for there is no deception."

We always think we know the truth, but almost always we do not know the whole picture. This is where non-judgment comes. How can we judge if we do not know? We even try to deceive ourselves by making excuses for doing things we would have done anyway without prompting.

How do we know the truth? Truth is in the NOW, without the stain of past nor the anticipation of the future.

Truth is your seeing the birds taking a bath in the water fountain and feeling that you yourself are feeling the coldness of the water and the lightness of the feathers as they shake the water off.

Truth is your child looking for his favorite shirt and instead of getting mad that he is old enough to take care of his clothes, seeing that it is not the shirt but what that shirt represented to him that is important NOW, not yesterday, not tomorrow, NOW. What is the use of getting mad?

Truth is knowing that the past is gone and what we have NOW are the lessons that we either learned or did not. Truth is the dogs nudging you to open the glass doors so they can go to the bathroom on your freshly mowed lawn.

To Command the Wind

A Shaman performs a ritual when there is no rain to sustain the crops in the village. An observer will think this ritual shrouded in myth and downright crazy, and yet he sees the rain come the following day. Not just drops, but lots and lots of it, and the fields are restored to life. One might say it was a coincidence, others will say it was just random chance. And yet another would say he commanded the wind to bring the rain with it.

In "The Lord of the Rings, The Fellowship of the Ring" Saruman tried to bring down the mountain and so fellowship had to re- route to the city of the dwarves.

Having grown up in an upland farm where water was scarce, I had paid particular attention to the smell of the air when I was a young child. I could sense when rain was coming. We planted rice and rain during certain periods of time rain was absolutely necessary. Irrigating the farm was out of the question.

My father always worried and when he did, I prayed that rain would come so that the fields would be watered. Most of the time, it did. Other times, it did not. When it came, everyone rejoiced. I remembered having the idea of luxury as building one of those gigantic water tanks which stored large amounts of rain water enough to use for a few months. I did not like it when my father had to cart water from a well two miles away to use for our daily needs.

I love the smell of the earth when rain was about to come. I had forgotten how it is. I had been educated and trained as a scientist and was mired in the world of believing only what I observed.

The other day, a fellow scientist told me he was holding a note on his hand and he lost it, and it was with a sense of awe and amusement at himself when he was telling me this. The bill was not on the floor, there was no one else close to him, he distinctly remembered holding it in his hand while it was still in his pocket, he looked at the floor, and it was not there.

As I was cleaning the table of much unnecessary paper that was there, I found a note, a large one. Equivalent to what he apparently lost. There was only one thing odd. His bill was in british pounds and mine was in US dollars.

Now I am back to when I was a child, believing everything is possible, as it should always be, as it is.

The Color of Kindness

"We can start working with time, if you wish, till you can fly the past and the future. And then you will be ready to begin the most difficult, the most powerful, the most fun of all. You will be ready to BEGIN to fly up and know the meaning of kindness and of love" -Chiang to Jonathan, after Jonathan has mastered space. In "Jonathan Livingston Seagull" by Richard Bach.

I was 14 years old when I read this book. So fascinated was I that I memorized phrases from it. Somehow it seemed to me to mean something other than a seagull wanting to fly fast that he was willing to leave his flock and be alone. Learn alone. Definitely more than that.

Even then I thought, how odd, that Chiang would say this when Jonathan had already perfected flight, and has mastered space. I thought, huh? Begin to learn the meaning of kindness and of love? It was not the learning part that confused me. Intuitively I knew we all have to learn it. Our parents teach it, the schools teach it, our spiritual leaders teach it., it was the "begin" part that baffled me. Why? You would think after all that time, he has learned it already.

Only after many years of meditation did I finally have a glimpse of what he meant. A glimpse.

The usual interpretation of kindness has some giver and receiver, a gift to be given, usually from someone who has something to give another. An implied hierarchy of power.

It is yellow when we extend it and think: " I am richer It than you are so take it." It is blue when we think : "It will make me feel good to extend it to you."It is green when we think : "Someday I would like you to extend this kindness back to me" It is red when we think : "I want you to love me."

True kindness is like a transcendent light that is on all the time, it has no flame and cannot burn, more like a radiator of heat. It is there. Period.

When action is required, it is given. When no action is required, it is still there. Actually true kindness and imperturbable peace are inseparable from each other.

I brought this topic up because all the books tell you you must give, give, give and I agree, but when you do, you must examine the frame of mind that you are in.

As long as you are caught up in dualistic notions, where there is a giver and a receiver, then the act of giving itself binds you. This is why Asvagosha advocates absolutely no gift giving or receiving for yoga practice.

So here is an exercise: Take the largest bill you can find from your pocket or purse. Begin transferring the bill from your left hand to your right hand, and then vice-versa. You would feel silly at first, but that is the whole purpose of the exercise.

When you extend kindness to another, there should be no giver or receiver perceived. You are merely transferring a thought, an intention or a material thing from your left hand to the other hand and vice versa.

When you can do this, give, and give generously.

Our Lives As Perfection in Motion

Your life, my life and everyone else's is Perfection in motion. You liken it to a stream. You put a boulder of rock on that stream and the water gets divided at the point where you put the boulder but at some point the water unites again. It does not matter how many boulders or small stones you put. You divide the water at those points, but the water unites regardless.

You and I put the rocks in our lives. We create the drama because we want to experience it. Now if we can just say, no, no more boulders or rocks, I am tired of the drama, then the water flows freely and fast as it was meant to be. Our lives are meant to be this way. The primitive mind does not accept it. It is much too simple. Simple truths are like that.

Up until I left the academic world, I had never had a job outside of the laboratory. It was the only world I knew. It was one of the things I enjoyed the most, working in the laboratory. Working in the laboratory is like composing a symphony. Every step in the experiment process has to be perfectly coordinated with the next step. Otherwise you waste time, talent, energy and money.

When it was time to choose where to go for my postdoctoral training, it was not easy. I chose to be in San Diego. Looking back, would I have had a different life now? I will never know. All I know is that through all those journeys, I found my life purpose. My conditioned mind tells me that it was not easy. I know now that it was necessary as I had not yet learned my lesson.

What is the use of looking back? We forge ahead and move forward, no longer burdened by the past. The hardest task you will ever have to do is to find your life's purpose. Sometimes the route to getting there is not easy. We get confused, blinded and sidetracked by our upbringing, mass mentality, our parents indoctrination.

We value tradition, honor our parents as we would any other person, because they have always been a part of our paths. We can choose to be aware or repeat karmic dramas again and again. Superimposed with the mini-dramas that we experience on a daily basis is a cosmic dance, always perfect, never missing a beat, always joyful, always beautiful.

But we are here in this lifetime in order to honor our karmic commitments, our sacred contracts- the ones that we made before we came back- that we may help others and that we may allow them to help us. When we realize this, and we become aware of the movie behind the movie, the painting behind another painting, the music in the background, a scent that lingers long after the first burst, then our lives become easier, simpler, lighter.

In the grander scale of things, what does it matter that you have to wake up every morning early so that you can take your son to school because he refuses to walk a few blocks from the parking lot to the school entrance?

A small sacrifice to honor a sacred contract.

Trusting the Process of Manifestation

The manifestation process works. The Universal laws are impersonal. Everyone is subject to the same laws. Just as the sun shines on everyone, the laws do not distinguish between the pious and the atheists, the beautiful and the plain, the good and the bad.

The caveat is the truth that we reap that which we sow and therefore what we do to others will always come back to us, one way or another, either in this lifetime or the next. This is the underlying principle behind the golden rule and this is the reason we do not try to harm others knowingly and willingly.

Our definitions are created only by our small mind and at one point or another we will find out that we are all One. But that is another story for some and another lifetime for another. We are all responsible for the consequences of our actions until we are free and then the karmic rules no longer apply.

When one asks me why it does not seem to work for them, or why it is taking them so long, I ask them to look within and see what is preventing them from having what they want. If it is good for you in the long run, it will come. If it is not good for you in the long run, then it will not. The safety valve is always on.

The analogy will be similar to that of the American Indian tribes. When a warrior does not catch a buffalo, the Shaman asks him to cleanse himself. He does not give reasons such as: the weather is bad, the buffaloes are hiding, someone else got there before me. Those are excuses.

When a Samurai sustains an injury from a fight, it is never because the other warrior is better or more skilled than himself in fighting. It is the same with everything. All the answers are within. Therefore seek the answers within.

On the one hand to take that kind of responsibility is empowering, on the other, it is also very scary. Authentic power is never bestowed, it is discovered within the Self. It is not dependent on your bank balance, your position in life, how many people love you. Those are all impermanent and can disappear in an instant. Seek that which is eternal and unbounded. It is your true nature.

Authentic power is the acknowledgment that the outside world is but a reflection of what goes on inside of us. This is the reason we work on ourselves. To find that our true nature is limitless, boundless and perfect.

This is the same reason one of the exercises I give ALL of my coaching clients is to look at themselves in the mirror, look at their eyes in the reflection and say "I love you and accept your for everything that you are."

Ultimately you will have to trust yourself, completely. You will have to let go of everything that you thought would make you secure. This means everything that no longer serves your higher good, you will have to let go. You can do it willingly, by awareness brought about by the narrow path of discipline either by meditation or by contemplation or prayer, or you are forced to let go of them by pain, in which case you will have to relearn the lessons of this lifetime, again.

Ironically, it is when you let go of your parachute that you'll discover you have wings.

The Alchemy of Emotions

According to the Merriam-Webster Dictionary, alchemy means the following:

1 : a medieval chemical science and speculative philosophy aiming to achieve the transmutation of the base metals into gold, the discovery of a universal cure for disease, and the discovery of a means of indefinitely prolonging life 2 : a power or process of transforming something common into something special 3 : an inexplicable or mysterious transmuting

When we talk about the alchemy of emotions we will use all three definitions.

There is a whole gamut of emotions that we humans have to relate to, on the path of self realization. An emotion is a conscious mental reaction. When combined with energy, it becomes feeling and it becomes very powerful.

To begin to touch heaven, we must first feel the earth. This is what the Buddha did when he became enlightened. He said "The earth is my witness."

Emotions are our earthly companions. For as long as we are here, we will have them. They are our shadows. We are their light.

To begin we must be aware of them at every moment. We know when we are getting annoyed, angry or sad. They do not come unannounced. We feel them. If we didn't then we have become one with them and there is no longer a necessity to relate to them. To relate to them we have to see the seeming duality between "us" and them.

The so called negative emotions we dislike and the positive emotions we encourage. This is where we feel trapped. Compassion, kindness and love we call positive emotions. Even love as we know it we have to relate to.

They are all emotions and can become vehicles to self knowledge. The truth is that they are all self directed. We only see that they are directed to someone else because we are habituated into thinking that. When we become completely honest with ourselves we see that the cause of any emotion is not the other person, but ourselves. It becomes very tricky.

To transmute anything, you have to have a handle on it.

Let us talk about the so called negative emotions first, for example, anger.

You feel angry about something or someone. You know this because you feel a constriction on your throat or a tightening of your stomach or blood rushing to your face. Your eyes squint. These are physical manifestations. The more important thing is that in your mind, you are absolutely certain you have been wronged. Something or someone hurt you.

You ask yourself, "Why am I angry?" Then you will come up with a reason and you keep exhausting the reason with "Why" and eventually, you will see that the anger is directed towards yourself. You have just performed discriminating awareness. To act out an anger is to escape that emotion. It is paradoxical but it is true.

Sadness is self pity. The bottom line is that you feel unloved and unworthy or you feel that you did not do enough. This is actually more dangerous than feeling angry. Everyone feels this way sometimes. It comes with being a human being. With the healthy individuals, it comes and then goes away. With some people this has become a habitual way of thinking and they need medication to alleviate it. Sometimes even medication is not enough.

I am a biochemist and know that there are centers in the brain that control the expression of these emotions so I have to clarify that these emotions are felt by those that are not clinically diagnosed. Only these feelings as they are experienced by the majority as a part of normal everyday life.

To sadness the answer is this. Just to be alive is a gift. Everything else is extra. You have transmuted sadness to gratitude.

Jealousy is a feeling that someone else has some attribute/thing/possession that you do not have. To this the answer is that there is no one like you on earth. You are unique and have to be happy about that uniqueness because it gives you a chance to contribute the best that you can. Yourself.

And now we can deal with the so called "positive" emotions. If we examine them, they lead to three things. An equilateral triangle of compassion, kindness, and wisdom. At the center of this triangle is love. Love, not the kind that we can qualify so easily, the point of convergence were I to draw a line across from one vertex to the center of the opposite line is pure love.

How many times have you fallen in love? It does not matter. The point is that in romantic love, the feeling passes unless it comes with compassion and kindness. Kindness that is selfless, compassion that is total, and in some instances, ruthless.

Pure love is what Jesus Christ is, what the realized sages are, what we are in truth, if we only work to peel off the layers upon layers of conditioning that we have been accustomed to from one lifetime to the next. To realize this is the only real quest worth pursuing.

Our Greatest Gift is Our Free Will

Free will is our greatest gift as a human being.

This the most critical piece of information you will ever need to remember. No person can will things for you, unless you surrender yours to that other person in which case you are giving away the greatest gift you have as a human being.

It would be the equivalent of Esau selling his birthright as a first born, to Jacob, for a meal.

This is the reason only in the human realm can one work towards the path of realization, even the gods get jealous of humans.

This is the same reason Jesus Christ did not bring us all up when he ascended.

This is the very same reason that when Buddha awakened, he could not awaken all of us. At first he did not want to come back to the world, but his compassion is so overwhelming that he did go back to teach those who were ready and let the others alone.

This is the same solution to the mystery of why when the sages awaken, they view the world as awakened but some of us remain ignorant until we learn our lessons.

To view others as awakened, first you have to have the eyes of an awakened person. And to that person our games maybe so humorous but he or she nevertheless understands and is so full of compassion that he or she is willing to work with you in your confused state of mind.

Because of the compassion that wells up in someone who awakes he or she would like to take everyone with him or her.

But this is a trap, for to take over someone's will, whether they give it to you willingly or not is a major violation of that person and immediately flings that master back to the pit of ignorance.

If you want to manifest anything, be it a material possession or awakening, you have to want it very much. There is energy in desire and you can use that energy if and only if you are able to focus it.

Unfocused energy is like wildfire. It can and will destroy everything in its path for it has no discernment.

We are in this world to experience all that we wanted before we were born and there is truth in these words:

"The world is so constructed, that if we wish to enjoy its pleasures, we must also endure its pains. Whether we like it or not, we cannot have one without the other." ~ Swami Brahmananda

So if you want to manifest anything in your life, you have to first identify it, get into a relaxed state, intend to have it, play a vision of having it in your mind and experience all that a sensory perception can experience.

There is no difference in actually having whatever it is in the physical realm or in the mental realm.

And then let it go. Letting it go means surrendering your conscious mind to that which is greater, you're higher Self, the part that is and will always be a part of God's, one that sees events way ahead of your limited conscious mind.
If it is good for you in the long run, it will come. But you have to trust. Take a leap of faith.

Detachment - A Key to Faster Manifesting

"When you want nothing, you can have everything". Wanting nothing means you already are in a state of having it. I realize that the most challenging step in manifesting a magical moment is detachment.

You intend, you visualize, and then you let it go and you repeat this process again and again until what you desire manifests in the material world.

There is a gap between the thought process and the actual manifestation in the physical world. That gap is your safety valve. In that gap,you can perfect the vision of what you have intended. After you have perfected the vision, you let it go. Much like encircling it in a bubble and then releasing it. We all have played with this when we were little. This is what detachment is about.

What detachment calls for is faith. Not blind faith but the intuitive knowledge that if something is good for you in the long run, it has to manifest.

The only discipline you need is sustained focus on that which you desire the most. However you also need to let go. To let it go, you need to go into the space of infinity where lies unlimited potential.

There is only one thing that the sages keep repeating in the books. There is nothing that is not contained in you. You simply have to access it. To access it, you need to be internally still. To be internally still is to trust. To trust in yourself.

I quote an excerpt of my book for those of you who have not yet read it.

Synopsis of My Journey to an Integrated Life

We look deep within and figure out what stirs our soul.

Once we make the decision of what is important in our lives, the universe opens up possibilities to get there, but we have to take a leap of Faith, wherever and however we find it, that we will be supported in our decision

Book Excerpt

The cube is a symbol of stability. It is also a symbol of total balance. Sometimes it is used to symbolize truth.

To me, the cube is a symbol of perfection, it is a symbol of an integrated life. An integrated life is a life led by an integrated person.

In it, there is perfect harmony between wants and needs, be they spiritual, financial, physical, mental or relationship needs and wants.

For each individual, such a perfect balance exists, and such balance can only be determined by the person living his or her life.

Paradoxically, achieving balance in all areas of our lives is not a static process but rather a very dynamic one. Our needs and wants change.

Everything outside of us changes. Our bodies change. How then do we achieve this balance when everything changes?

We must bring ourselves back to that which is immutable, our divine Self which is unchanging.

It is pure, perfect, endowed with infinite wisdom and has within it all the knowledge required to make sound decisions. All we have to do is remember it.

When we remember this Self, we are in the moment, and all of our thoughts and actions or inactions are perfect for that moment. An integrated life is a series of perfect moments, arranged like pearls in a necklace that has no clasps.

Clearing Blockages of Energy Centers

The heart is the energy center where all manifestation begins. This is why we say I wish with all my heart that...

It is possible to begin manifestation directly from the heart, to not deal with energies, if and only if one has already done the discipline of meditation or deep contemplation as in the case of saints. For everyone else who are just beginning, the following exercise is recommended to remove blockages in the body's energy conduit.

Before one begins, I must caution that this exercise has little to do with the Vehicle of direct energy, Tantra. For that both the Hinayana and the Mahayana vehicles must have been mastered. I am afraid there are no shortcuts. [For further reading, use Chogyam Trungpa's books, Meditation in Action, Cutting Through Spiritual Materialism and Shambhala: the Sacred Path of the Warrior]

We will simply call this exercise as clearing the path.

This exercise may propel you to activate kundalini and unless both the body and the mind are sufficiently purified, you may not be able to handle the surge of energy through your body. The most important part is to pay attention to the reaction of your body and then document it after the exercise. You may do this exercise standing up or sitting in half lotus or full lotus position.

Imagine yourself at the center of an hour-glass. Now imagine that your heart is at the center of that hour glass. This hour glass is unusual because the top is one half circle and the bottom is the other half circle.

The top looks like a wine glass with very short stem and is connected to the other half with that stem. That stem is where your heart is.

Now envision a flexible tube or cord that runs from the base of our spine to the center of the earth and you are now connected to the core of the earth. The base of your spine is the first Chakra. It is the color of the finest ruby. Red, not blood red but dark red and brilliant. This ruby red ball is floating right inside your spine and you can see it as pure as the finest ruby. No imperfections. Breathe through your first chakra and feel the energy coming from the center of the earth to your first chakra.

Follow the energy going from the first chakra to the second chakra which is 3 inches above the base of your spine. There is an orange ball there brilliant and pure, like an orange except that is luminous. Breathe three times into the brilliant orange ball.

Follow the energy to the area of the solar plexus, three inches below the navel. Breathe into it. This is the third chakra and its color is yellow, like the sun. Again you imagine that this yellow ball is floating inside the body not held by anything. Breathe into it three times.

Follow the energy from the third chakra into your heart center. The color of the ball is luminous green. Stay there. Breathe into it and through it. You can expand the green ball as much as you like. Feel it. Feel your heart center opening. Breathing in love, breathing out love. How does it feel?

Relax and get centered.

Now imagine that the energy is now going from your heart center into your throat area and that in that throat area is a blue ball just floating. The fifth chakra has the color blue like the deep blue ocean. Breathe into it three times. Follow the energy from the throat into the sixth chakra, which is your third eye. Again breathe into it and imagine that it opens little by little as you breathe into it. Like a baby's eyes the first time he wakes up in the morning.

Now imagine the energy flowing up from your sixth chakra into the crown of your head. Above the physical skull, a violet ball that symbolizes the awakened mind. Breathe into this ball three times. Pause.

Splitting the energy beam.

Imagine a beam of light coming from space. You see no beginning or end to this. The beam of light is like a laser beam of pure white light focused on the crown chakra. As it enters the crown chakra follow the flow of this light through all the centers as you breathe through all the centers, stopping at the root chakra.

When your attention is at the root chakra, imagine that the cord connecting you to the center of the earth is now connected to this energy flow which started from the crown of your head. There is now free exchange and continuous flow of energy up and
down. A dance. Your body has become a conduit of energy.

The last step is continuing the flow of energy from both ends, from both the root chakra connected to the center of the earth and from the crown chakra. This time the energy going into the crown chakra is used to create a spiral that envelopes your body and then the energy spiral which begun in the crown chakra now ends at the root chakra, merging with the energy from the cord and now simply going up the other centers.

Write the feeling after you do this meditation and keep a journal for all the times you meditate using this method.

Manifesting Magical Moments One Day at a Time

By | Submitted On May 13, 2009

As a scientist, I am able to do repetitive things hours at a time. It does not bore me. It is the same reason I am able to eat the same thing again and again and again. I do not crave for variety. Sometimes a single experiment has to be done within a stretch of ten hours. I was used to it. Every day, I see magic happen in my own life within a 24 hour stretch. Nothing spectacular, just little moments. Magic is a part of my life.

Last night was different. I was emailing a friend about and I told him three because I forgot to count the others. But as "A Course in Miracles" reiterated, there are no small miracles. All of them are weighted the same. First, I found a quarter at the gas pump. Considering that it is an everyday occurrence for me to find a penny, a nickel or a dime and sometimes multiples of them every single day, a quarter was a big deal. I put it in my wallet. It was the second quarter I found in three days.

Second, I got a call from four different investors from four different sites where I posted advertisements. One hundred percent response on a single ad.

Third, I made a client at least $25,000 instant profit on a single purchase. This was truly amazing. Fourth, I found the perfect tenant for one property that I am managing.
Fifth I lined up another tenant for another property making that property one hundred percent occupied.

Sixth, my gardener brought the right tools this time so he could trim the bushes, without my telling him. I simply wished it. Normally I would tell him and he would come back with the tools.

Seventh, I found an answer to a question, a very personal one. It was eye opening. It was as if a whole new world opened for me.

Here are the things that I did that day that I do not normally do.

I was so happy that I was laughing by myself, aloud, in the car, as I was remembering some things.

When I met with my clients, I put myself in their shoes. I already know what it is like to make these kinds of purchases, big ticket items, long term investments. I "removed" the pressure from them by being in their shoes and letting be. I repeated the phrase "Thy Will be Done."

Third, I relinquished all appearances of outward control. I was simply being. I simply acted on what was needed to be done at the moment.

Fourth, I did the Heart Meditation (see previous article on Clearing Blockages) once in the morning and once in the evening. I
had been up since four in the morning and never did I have so much energy.

The most important thing I did was I put myself in Sacred Space as often as I could. A bubble of unconditional Love. I let go. The key elements for manifesting: happiness, detachment, simply being and going into a space of unconditional love. In that space of unconditional love, there is no resistance, no expectation, no clinging, no wanting a desired outcome.

You are simply experiencing Love. Pure love. It is the space where all the magic happens.

I wish you as many or more magical moments in a day as you can handle. I hope that this would help you get what you desire the most.

How to Develop Fearlessness

By | Submitted On May 31, 2009

I remember having to spank my only child one day when he was really little. I was crying on the inside while I was doing it but it needed to be done. It was for his own good.

I had to write a quite difficult letter the other day. It was to cut off communications with someone I was, and still am, quite fond of. A beloved friend. I did not want to do it but it was necessary. I did not imagine the pain. The anguish was real. I felt it in my stomach and my tears flowed again, for the first time after I thought I had exhausted them during my meditations. It was, not only the pain of attachment to the other person, but also of attachment to what I thought I had transcended a long time ago. After all I had been meditating for twenty years. I am supposed to be beyond all of this.

I had to examine why it was painful. It was because I had to confront my own emotions, the ones that I consider improper and not worthy of me. Not only am I vain, I am also spiritually materialistic. The paradox is that as one becomes spiritually materialistic, it is the same time that one becomes spiritually bankrupt.

There are feelings that we categorize as "not belonging" to a spiritually mature individual: jealousy, rage, envy, thoughts of vengeance, possessiveness. These are considered "bad" feelings.

To develop fearlessness is to confront that which we fear face to face.

This is what is painful. When one decides that it is time to sever one's relationship to rejecting these feelings as bad, a radical severance is required. It is painful to cut through frivolity because we want to hang on to it. It is our nature to want to do so.

Frivolity comes in many forms, not necessarily as simple as vanity paying so much attention to how one looks physically. It could take the form of greed in the sense of spiritual progress. This is even more dangerous than simple vanity.

Just like an umbilical cord that needs to be cut, one has to have ruthless compassion towards oneself when using the Sword of Manjusri*. Above all else, it requires absolute honesty with oneself, to accept rather than shove under the rug, to be able to say yes they are there, these feelings and that they do not necessarily diminish oneself.

These feelings are thoughts, fueled with emotions, but when we relate to them fully we find that just like everything else, they pass. To reject them is to empower them and to empower them is to not recognize the fact that like everything else, they are an avenue to freedom.

On the one hand, while it is painful to acknowledge these emotions, facing them with the Sword of Manjusri allows one to do the right thing for oneself- to realize that to progress on the path to freedom, one has to cut through frivolities, not of one's relationship with others but with oneself, and to transmute the fiery nature of emotions.

To become fearless is to reclaim authentic power and to know that everything, every event, every person that we meet, we created in order to usher us to absolute freedom. We invited them there at the deepest level because in the more encompassing view, our objective is to realize that only our thoughts separate us from others.

So we acknowledge that the other person or event was not the cause of anger, it is rather oneself rejecting feelings as they come and questioning why they arise when one is supposed to be above them.

We accept that we have them, we do not hang on to them, we do not act on them, rather we observe them. This is discriminating awareness.

And we give thanks for all that there was and hope that in some way we have enriched someone else's life if only for a short time, and that to let them grow, we have to respect their free will and honor their paths.

*Manjusri is the god of discriminating awareness. In the Buddhist literature, his flaming sword is the symbol of wisdom and ruthless compassion, the one that cuts through all duality, arrogance and frivolity.

Discipline is the Only Way to Freedom

According to the Merriam-Webster dictionary online, discipline means the following:

dis·ci·pline
Function: noun
Etymology: Middle English, from Anglo-French & Latin; Anglo-French, from Latin disciplina teaching, learning, from discipulus pupil

Date: 13th century

1: Punishment
2: Obsolete : instruction
3: A field of study
4: Training that corrects, molds, or perfects the mental faculties or moral character
5 a: Control gained by enforcing obedience or order b: Orderly or prescribed conduct or pattern of behavior c: self-control
6: A rule or system of rules governing conduct or activity

A Samurai practices with his sword fighting techniques, everyday. A monk sits in meditation every day. A pious person prays every day. A world class athlete trains everyday for an event one year ahead.

Jesus Christ prayed and fasted for forty days. Even the Buddha sat in meditation after realizing enlightenment.

This is what discipline is about. It is the ability to will yourself into doing what does not come easy, for a higher purpose, a goal that you want to achieve. It requires conscious choice and in that conscious choice is intent.

There is value in repetitive tasks. It quiets the mind of chatter. Being able to do something repetitively involves the discipline to do it day after day.

Chogyam Trungpa once said, in order to go to depths of meditation, one has to first be able to sit and relate to the boredom and the simplicity of meditation. Just follow your breath. When one is able to relate to the boredom then all of the last four definitions of discipline are fulfilled.

The progression of the path to freedom goes : From discipline, knowledge, from knowledge, understanding, from understanding, awareness, from awareness, detachment, from detachment, freedom.

In the case of the manifestation process, the discipline required is the ability to focus on what you want rather than being bogged down and discouraged by what you see outside of you.

Discipline yourself to see what is good, in every moment and to see that your life really is perfection in motion. There is no one else who can do it for you. I can force feed someone. They do not have to swallow it. If they did choose to swallow it, they are still the ones who will have to digest the food. If it were possible for someone to do it for us, we would not reap the benefit of it. The consequence of discipline is freedom. The price of freedom is discipline.

If we are to transcend this world, as in what Jesus Christ meant when he said "To be in this world but not of it" then we have to accept the following saying of an unknown sage:

"The World is so constructed that if we wish to enjoy its pleasures, we must also endure its pains. Whether we like it or not, we cannot have one without the other."

A Simple Technique to Reclaim Your Authentic Power

I have only worked with two long term clients as a coach. By long term I mean one hour every week for more than 12 months. The results of those coaching sessions are so remarkable that I will share them with you. In both instances, as a coach, I am not allowed to dictate what the clients have to do.

To dictate is to dis-empower if not to un-empower. Always choose to empower another for in so doing, you empower yourself in more ways than the limited mind can create.

In our sessions I only showed them how to change a way of thinking so that eventually they realized that they create everything in their lives.

No outside force. The important thing is to "FEEL" the difference between attributing an outside circumstance as the cause of our predicament and taking responsibility for whatever occurred.
1. " I allowed myself to be upset by what my wife said."

2. "Subconsciously, I wanted to leave that job. I did not love my job, I was staying there to put food on the table but I realized that that job is not the only thing I can do so having to leave that job was a blessing, although it did not feel like it at that time."

Behind every word is a thought. The word is a vehicle, no more. However since we are so thoroughly indoctrinated in a habitual thought pattern we are not even aware of it, we have to do it the other way around. This is the essence of Neuro Linguistic

Programming. We say the word, we create the thought, the neurons are fired and a new thought pattern is embedded. This is why affirmations work.

Say the words, feel the words and know the new thought pattern it has created. Here are common exercises.
Finish each sentence as you please

I don't want to
I would like to
I would rather
I probably can
I prefer to
I choose to
I intend to
I can and I will

A few key points. Words are vehicles. They are created from thought. We are accustomed to thinking a certain way so we need to change the pattern of thinking by playing with the words, which creates a new thought pattern and with it a certain feeling. It is by feelings that we communicate to the universe.

You can not request the universe for a home on the beach in La Jolla if in the back of your mind you are thinking "Oh, but how am I going to regenerate the 8 figures required to afford a home there? Answer, if you had it before you can have it again. No doubt." Get the picture?

One last note. You don't become happy because of material things. You get material things because you chose to be happy and in that space of happiness is the seed for manifestation of every material desire one can have. So choose to be happy first, then everything else will follow.

How to Reverse a Habitual Pattern of Thought in Order to Manifest

"Break the chains of your thoughts,and you break the chains of your body too." ~Richard Bach "Jonathan Livingston Seagull"

To change a habit, we must first change our thoughts.

I love the sitcom "Seinfeld". It is truly creative, witty and funny. A show about life. I can watch the episodes again and again and again, just like I can watch the old Star Trek Series, any episode, again and again. To me everything that the characters in Seinfeld encountered was so real and that is how life is. It is full of unexpected moments. Life can be viewed as tragic or comical. I choose the latter.

There was one particular episode that I can remember playing in my head. It was when George decided that for one day, he would be a winner. I never really understood his predicament until after I asked a friend why it was so funny that he lived with his parents. In the Philippines, that would be so common. In America, to be living with parents after a certain age is not at all cool. My friend blatantly said one is considered a loser when this happens. That is the perception of the people outside.

So in this episode, George said, "Just for today, I am going to be a winner" He approached the most beautiful woman sitting in the bar and boldly declared: "Hi, I'm George. I am 37 years old and I live with my parents." He got the girl and pretty much for that week everything seemed to go well with him. And then they went back to normal. What it was before. Why? In the show, it is what life is. Things go well and then they go back to where they were before.

Analyzing this situation in the context of habitual thought patterns, George asserted himself, for a while. And then he went back to his old way of thinking and so consequently he went back to the way his life was, before. Same old George.

It is never easy to change a habitual way of thinking. Sometimes we are so used to it that we don't even know we are doing it. This I know from experience. It is this habitual way of thinking that imprisons us, paralyzes us and keep us from realizing our true potential. In the manifestation process, this sprouts as doubt. Doubt about yourself, doubt about your worthiness to receive, doubt about why you can when you have not before. The answer, you can NOW!

One way to do this is to watch yourself in a film for the following day. You make the script and you also direct. Record your observations and FEELINGS for that day, then you can always go back to it when you forget. We always do. Why ? We want to go back to the familiar because it is comfortable As long as we are unable to go beyond what is comfortable, we will never progress.

A caveat. For every material thing we wish to manifest, there is a deeper, more basic reason we desire it. It is the call of the soul for something. It is that which we want to manifest. For the advanced practitioners, they bypass the material desire and go directly to that which the soul longs for.

How to Capture Miraculous Moments, Magical Moments

"I know the joy of fishes in the river through my own joy as I walk along the river"-from the "Joy of Fishes, in The Way of Chuang Tzu" by Thomas Merton

To be in Tao is to be in the Flow all the Time. However this state of mind is only arrived at either after a long time of self discipline or after eons of being reincarnated, either way, one has to go through the tests, of will, of character, of spiritual tenacity and at times, what reason calls the verge of madness. This is what St. John of the Cross calls the dark night of the soul. To be in the flow all the time means to be in absolute surrender to the present moment, whatever is called for.

The discipline required is of the will, man's will. In time, there can be absolute surrender but to get there and stay there one has had to have dissected the ego and realize it for what it is: a construct of the mind that has become master. It is so intelligent it does not want to be a slave, it wants to enslave instead.

When one is in the flow then every moment is truly magical. In this state of mind, when all resistances are given up, surrendered, one can manifest and sometimes, instantaneously.

And yet there are moments that we are in the flow and yet still not recognize it.

I will tell you three stories of manifesting magical moments. One is about one of my clients, and the other two about two of my friends.

This one is about the power of intention/decision/desire

One of my business clients wanted a modest estate for a new home. He had found so many to look at but his heart was set on this one. He wanted it. It was his hearts' desire.

To my amazement and pure delight, he created a situation where the unusual became possible. When on the verge of getting it, he decided he did not want it after all.

This is a real life situation. The fascinating thing about it from my point of view is the ability of one man to desire something so much that his desire fueled a series of events that would lead to what he THOUGHT he wanted and then decided he did not.

It reminds me of the episode where Spock's future wife created a situation where she would end up the victor regardless of what happens, and Spock telling her in the end that "You will find that having is not the same as wanting."

The second one is more radical.

It is "Instantaneous Manifestation of Desire"

One of my friends lost her car to an accident and the insurance she had did not cover for a replacement.

For two weeks she tells me "Oh, Melinda, I could really use a car right now. I really need a car, I want a car but I do not have the money to buy one right now"

I told her "So manifest a car. Having the money to buy the car is an extra step. There are many ways for you to get the car" Three days of my telling her this.
She writes me the third day and says "Melinda, one of my friends got promoted and will be having a nice company car. He told me I can have his old car!"

The lesson:"Ask for what you want and forget about how it will come to you" Once she "believed" that she could have the car without the money, the car came.
The third one we experience, often, but do not pay attention to it so much because we attribute it to chance.

One of my friends needed a computer but he did not have much money. He decided that he will get a computer with everything for what he can afford to pay $200.

One week he searched. There was only one listed that was selling for $200. He called the person and the computer for sale was two years old and had all the programs I myself had paid for over a thousand dollars for my own computers. The guy who
owned it is a techie and just wanted to get rid of his two year old computer Miraculous for my friend and yet when he was telling me about it, he attributed it to chance.

What will it be for you? Your task is to pay attention

There is an easier way, a shortcut if you will. Capture the feeling of loving unconditionally and from that viewpoint, ask, create, desire what you want and then let it go.

Allow the Universe to bring you what you want. It works.

If what you want is for your own highest good, it will ALWAYS work.

I wish you everything your heart desires, always, but only if it is good for you in the long run, and that is why we always end any manifestation session with

"I know it will come to me under the best circumstances and at the proper time if it is for my best and highest good, and if it is for the best and highest good of everyone involved. I give thanks in advance and I can simply let it go."

How to Align Your Life Vision With Your Soul Purpose

I dreamed of winning the Nobel Prize when I was in college. It did not seem to be so lofty at the time. After all I was with the best minds of my time, the kids who ate Friedrich Nietzsche for breakfast. I set my goals to working for five years to send my younger brother to school, going to graduate school and then on to winning the Nobel in Chemistry and or Physiology and Medicine.

My father died a few months before I graduated from college. It was more traumatic to me than anything I could have imagined. I buried the pain. I did not even cry at his funeral.

I knew he still would have wanted everything else for me and I focused on all the plans I had made. They did not pan out. It turned out I was only meant to work for two years, apply for graduate school in only one school, got accepted and left my job. I crossed continents and for the first time I was away from my family. It was a shock to my system to move to another country.

In graduate school, while getting my Master's degree, it was not as I envisioned it to be. My supervisor insisted that I wash my own dishes so I stayed till 2 am in the laboratory sterilizing the used glassware, cooling them and setting them in the dishwasher so that I would have glassware to use the following morning.

This experience was entirely new to me. I had people who prepared everything I needed for my experiments while I was working, so really all I had to do was show up and do the experiments. I felt that. I had a hard time and although I so missed my parents and wanted to go home to the Philippines. It was not an option. I could not go home without a degree. It would disgraceful not for me but for my mother. I could not do it.

And then a miracle! In graduate school I fell in love, got married and forgot all about my dream. I only wanted to raise a family of my own. The Nobel was no longer a desire. While I was married, having nothing else to do while waiting for my ex husband to finish his degree, I enrolled in the Ph.D. program. This time I had fun. My studies were always second to my role as a wife and I simply enjoyed being in school. And then my marriage fell apart

And then my son came. My whole world was turned upside down. I had been divorced for over a year, not done with my dissertation and all alone.

In all these times I counted on the grace and kindness of all the people around me. They were heaven sent.

I spent many years trying to reconcile everything that had happened in my life. That quest was almost always wrought with pain. My ego was so thick, I could hardly see through it.

It is only a few years before writing this that I have discovered my own soul aligned purpose. I was not born to win the Nobel in Chemistry or in Physiology and Medicine. I am here only so that my son can be raised the way he was raised. Not a very lofty purpose, but nevertheless, real.

Once I have accepted this with everything else that it implied, life did not become easier but it did become more spacious.

I could finally appreciate the warmth of the sun on my face and the brush of cold wind on my cheeks, not from the ski resorts in Colorado but right behind my backyard.

I have no more lofty goals other than to see that my son is happy with his chosen path. All those years of struggle boiling down to a single purpose, to take care of my son and take the role of both father and mother to him.

The lesson, as long as what one is doing is not aligned with the soul purpose, it will be a life of struggle and pain, of ceaseless journey between the realms of the gods, the jealous god, the human realm, the animal realm and the hell realms as mentioned in most Buddhist literature.

How do you know what your life purpose is? You need to examine the life you have lived and see where the pain came from and what you learned from those painful experiences.

We were not meant to live a life of pain and struggle. Those were experiences that you either chose or were directed to because you were not paying attention to what is required of you.

This self examination requires absolute honesty but without judgment on our part. You may want to write down your insights to the following questions.

1. What periods of my life were the happiest? Why?

2. What periods of my life were the saddest? Why?

3. Was there a repeating pattern in my life which I chose to ignore and yet keep presenting itself?

4. To what end can I use my unique abilities, skills and talents that will allow me to be both self fulfilled, happy and of help to those that are in my life right NOW?

5. What unique contribution can I do to the world at large?

6. How can I fit my current circumstances to what I have discovered about myself?

You may ask "What has my soul purpose got to do with my career?"The answer is everything. Your work is such an integral part of your daily life and if it does not make you happy then there is a misalignment somewhere and you need to figure it out. Keep on working on yourself and know that you are always guided and that the Universe will always support you if what you are doing is in alignment with your soul purpose.

Exercises

Anchoring as a Means to Groundedness

As a coach, I am not allowed to tell my clients what to do, as I have not the right to take away their power to choose their course of action. I can give examples and the one that always comes to mind is when the Buddha talked to a grandmother who told him that she too wishes to be enlightened, however, she does not have the time to sit down and meditate since she is responsible for too many people.

I compare her to the CEO of a corporation or the Principal Investigator in a research laboratory, or a mother who has to take care of her children, earn a living, keep house, take care of aging parents, attend to other siblings and so on and so on.

Our responsibilities will always be there, especially knowing that we are the writer, director and producer of our lives.

We choose the roles that we play and we choose to create the movies of our lives. When we have chosen these roles, there is still a means to anchor ourselves, to be grounded in our being. For example, as we take showers, we can say "As I cleanse this body, may I also cleanse my mind", "As I brush my teeth, may I also brush the dust off my mind", "As I scrub this floor, may I also clean my thoughts".

When one wishes to apply this to material creation, then one can use it to remind himself or herself that material thing he or she wishes to manifest. For example as one drinks tea in the morning, one can say "I, (your name) now have (the object that one desires)and then get into the feeling of having what it is that one desires. The key is to be present in the here and now.

Grounding is a means to realize ourselves and we can use physical actions as anchors towards getting that which we desire, no matter what it is that we desire.

How to Appreciate the Present Moment

I can remember taking my son back home when he was born. I had to leave him in the hospital for a few days to have his body temperature stabilize.

Oh I had such great expectations of motherhood. I bought all cotton diapers determined that I will be "eco friendly"...This lasted two days.

I was in the process of writing my dissertation. I thought, well, I have a computer at home, I only have a couple of more experiments to do, it will be a breeze.

It was bliss. I loved taking care of him. I almost always put my head on his heart when he slept. He slept so soundly. There was only one problem, he slept soundly for an hour or two and then he would wake up again. Because of lack of sleep, my head was empty and there was nothing I could write about.

I would read the sentences I wrote and would be incredulous that I even wrote it.

I had to make one of the hardest decisions in my life. To either take him home to the Philippines for my family to take care of him while I finish my doctorate, or we can both go home together to the Philippines and have my family take care of both of us.

I chose the first one.

That was eighteen years ago. Today we were talking about a girl. How does he determine whether he wants her from the ego's standpoint or from the heart. The answer was not easy.

If it is from the heart then he would be happy for the girl regardless of whether she is with him or not, as long as the girl is happy. If it is from the ego, he would want to possess the girl and would be very unhappy if she chose someone else, and in this case, she had many other boys to choose from. She happens to be the most popular girl in school.

Taking my son back to the Philippines was truly a yesterday, like a lifetime ago, but even my going to the supermarket this afternoon to get his favorite dessert, is also a yesterday. It is done,in the past.

The NOW is when the past, present and future converge.

We can not undo the past. No one can. And yet for the majority of us, we hang on to the past hurts, past victories.

We are almost always trapped by it.

If we could only see that NOW is when we have the power to create, to be fully in the NOW is the only objective of our life, and that our future is created in the NOW, we would always welcome the saying 'Say Goodbye to Yesterday' even if it happened only a few minutes back. In this moment lies all the power your can handle.

How to Be Internally Quiet

There are so many techniques that are offered us in order to manifest something, so many tools, and the most important of them all is internal silence.

In the silence you can hear the sound of creation. In many traditions, it is AUM, but it is not the sound that we hear when we buy a CD or a tape. There are many stages prior to one's hearing this sound. First, the buzzing of a bee and then a bird twittering, then the sound of a flute, a harp, harpsichord, and finally, one day, one glorious day, the sound of creation.

It is unmistakable because it is followed by profound peace, and just like anything else, it is only momentary.

This is not to say that only the chanting of the mantra can bring us there. For the mystics, after passing through "the dark night of the soul" as St. John of the Cross had written beautifully, they did hear it as well.

I will only quote what is in the bible because it is what is readily available to me as I write this, and will not go into a discussion of a personal God. This concept of a personal God seems to be a subject of contention for centuries.

"John 1: 1-14"

1 In the beginning was the Word, and the Word was with God, and the Word was God.
2 The same was in the beginning with God.
3 All things were made by him; and without him was not anything made that was made.
4 In him was life; and the life was the light of men.
5 And the light shineth in darkness; and the darkness comprehended it not.
6 There was a man sent from God, whose name was John.
7 The same came for a witness, to bear witness of the Light, that all men through him might believe
8 He was not that Light, but was sent to bear witness of that Light.
9 That was the true Light, which lighteth every man that cometh into the world.
10 He was in the world, and the world was made by him, and the world knew him not.
11 He came unto his own, and his own received him not.
12 But as many as received him, to them gave the power to become the sons of God, even to them that believe on his name:
13 Which were born, not of blood, nor of the will of the flesh, nor of the will of man, but of God.
14 And the Word was made flesh, and dwelt among us, (and we beheld his glory, the glory of the only begotten of the Father,) full of grace and truth."

The sound of creation is what we hear when the tumult of the mind is quieted.

In that space, there is no resistance, no memory of the past which holds us back. It is what we experience when we are so focused on what we are doing at the moment that we forget time. We get lost in time.

It is what we experience when we are in Samadhi, deep meditation but even deep meditation is not enough. The real aim of meditation is to create peace, moment by moment.

It is only when we are peaceful that we are connected to "What IS"

In this state, we are perfectly aligned with the universal creative mind, and like the computer in Star Trek, we can say "Computer, coffee with little cream and sugar" and the computer will make it for us, just as we like it.

How to Clarify What You Want

We are often so busy with the day to day activities that we forget to nurture the inner child within. We have forgotten the dreams of our childhood and more important, we have forgotten who we are. When we were young we thought everything was possible. We need to go back to that time.

This exercise will allow you to both identify what you want and make it clearer to you. It will cover all aspects of your life, both spiritual and material.

You need a time when you can be by yourself, free from all distractions of the outside world. If that requires that you lock yourself in one of the bathrooms in the house, then do so. The point being this is a time for YOU.

The most important requirement for this exercise is to go back to the time when you were really happy, so before proceeding to do the exercise, please take a moment to remember such a time and put yourself there. Remember the feeling. If you have the luxury of being alone in the home and will be undistracted for a while, then you can put on some music that really makes you happy.

It will be much better if you are out in the fresh air, feeling the earth below you and seeing the heavens above, but it is all up to you. Above all else, no judgment. Do not judge what you write.

When you are ready, you can begin.

You will need several sheets of papers 8.5 x 11 inches.

Fold the sheet lengthwise then draw a line where you have it folded.

Your areas of focus are:

Spiritual Development
What would you do to enhance your spiritual development? This is all very personal and you need not elaborate on it for anyone but yourself.

Health
What would you like to have or experience in terms of health?
What is your definition of healthy?

Family
How would you improve your family relationships?

Relationships: friendships, romance
What would your ideal romance and friendly relationships be like?

Personal Achievements
Make a list of all the things you have ever wanted to do

Money
This area is very sensitive. Only you can define it. The most important question is "What would I give in terms of service and or product that will allow me to create the kind of money that would make me comfortable?"

Your Unique Contribution to the World

You are a unique individual but you live in this world. We all do. Part of your being here is to make a contribution to the world at large. It is your dharma, your role in life, your path, in this lifetime.

You can add another category if you like.

Put the categories/labels at the very top of each sheet ON THE LEFT HAND SIDE in bold. Write everything you want on the left hand side and what you do not want on the right hand side.

It is important that you clarify both not wants and wants so as you write on the left hand side you need to write something on the right hand side.

This exercise when done properly will take a while.

When you are done, use scissors to cut out the right hand side. Shred it or tear it out, or better yet, burn it.

Carry the left hand side of your list with you or put it in a place where you will see it at least once a day.

How to Communicate Well

There are many forms of communication. In this hub I will only talk about speech/verbal communication.

My son has an English vocabulary three times the size of mine. Sometimes I am awed by the big words he uses and I ask him what they mean. Sometimes I am too proud to ask, so I just look up the meaning. At all times, I ask him in what context he uses the words.

It is quite a delightful challenge to have an everyday dokusan* with a Zen Master who does not know he is one, yet. He is still a very typical american teenager.

He calls it verbal combat and with me, he always wins. He is a champion debater.

There can be no perfect communication, the best we can hope for is to have a very high degree of transmission of information between people.

The moment the information leaves the other person it is already flawed. It is impossible to communicate the thoughts/feelings that prompted the statement.

Our perception is colored by our experiences. These are called filters. We filter the information through a lens built by our upbringing, childhood, our ancestral and cultural heritage, the people we have interacted with.

There are a few things that we can do to enhance the communication process.

First, we acknowledge the possibility that the other person may not understand us perfectly. Second, we allow a space, a gap, where anything can happen. We let go of the desire to be understood, to influence, convince the other person of our point of view. We state the facts as we see them. We remove aggression altogether.
Third we allow the other person to take what we say as he sees it through his own filter. As for non verbal cues, we look them in the eye.

When we do this we communicate our sincere desire to communicate, no matter how imperfect. We acknowledge the other person, just as he or she is.

*a dokusan is a verbal combat between a Zen Master and a student. It aims to determine the state of consciousness of the student. A master will ask the student a question and the answer is never the logical answer to the question.

The main block to our communication is our consciousness of ourselves. If we put attention, full attention to the other person, we would listen better, the other person will be more comfortable and will listen more to us. Try it..

Immediately there is an improvement in the process.

Finally, if it is public speaking that you are interested in learning, the key is practice, practice, practice.

Other forms of communication: Telepathic communication, Intuition.

Our dogs can tell me when they are hungry, when they want to go to the bathroom, when they want simple attention and when they are annoyed by simply looking at me or wagging their tail.

They do not have to make a sound at all.

You can write love letters or you can also communicate telepathically.

It is not a myth.

How to Cultivate Awareness

Awareness, in the spiritual sense, means taking into account the totality of the environment one is part of.

According to Merriam-Webster

Main Entry: aware Pronunciation: \ans-'wer\Function: adjectiveEtymology: Middle English iwar, from Old Englishgewær, from ge- (associative prefix) + wær wary — more at co-, waryDate: before 12th century

1 archaic : watchful, wary
2 : having or showing realization, perception, or knowledge

— aware?ness noun

synonyms aware, cognizant, conscious,sensible, alive, awake mean having knowledge of something. aware implies vigilance in observing or alertness in drawing inferences from what one experiences <aware of changes in climate>. cognizant implies having special or certain knowledge as from first hand sources <not fully cognizant of the facts>.conscious implies that one is focusing one's attention on something or is even preoccupied by it <conscious that my heart was pounding>. sensible implies direct or intuitive perceiving especially of intangibles or of emotional states or qualities <sensible of a teacher's influence>. alive adds to sensible the implication of acute sensitivity to something

<alive to the thrill of danger>. awake implies that one has become alive to something and is on the alert <a country always awake to the threat of invasion>.

/watch?

Most of the time we are simply doing our habits. The life that we have or assumed we have is a consequence of the past. Past memories, programming, implants,suggestions, conditioning, giving us a sense of solidity. With solidity comes boundaries, and with boundaries, territories.

In the animal kingdom, the animals act by instinct. They do what they can to survive. Man, because of his assumed boundaries brought by his consciousness is still an animal by instinct, but the consciousness dictates that he protects his territory, his boundaries.

From this illusion of separation from the rest, I, me, mine arise. Some people are happy with what they have.They live their lives instinctively in this world without the need to dominate others.

Others feel the need to expand their territories and from this arises greed, envy, jealousy, hatred, anger.

The process of meditation allows us to relate to the moment as it is. No past or future, only now. From it comes the awareness that while we are part of a whole, the whole lives in us. This is affirmed by being aware of the breath.

Very simply being aware of our breath is meditation. It allows us to go to the gap. In the gap, there is nothing.

Going deeper into meditation we see the great void. Nothingness. No space, no time. In this gap, you realize, you are not who you thought you were. In this gap, there is peace. In this gap, there is only union.

To get there the first time, the ego will try to scare us into coming back. There is no way to get past that scare other than manual labor. You sit, sit, sit, whether you like it or not, and then, you know when you have reached past the ego when there is no longer a need to get up.

You have no desire to get up and be active. You have no desires, period, and there is no memory of the past, nor a hope for the future. There is only now and you experience it. You are at one with the here and now, and with everything and everyone around you in this phenomenal world.

Sooner or later we have to go this route. There is no other way. We can do all kinds of self improvement techniques to bypass it, but those are simply sidetracks. We can prolong this sidetrack as long as we like. We can even go back to the point where we want to undo everything.

I remember this quote while Cypher was talking to Agent Smith in "The Matrix". He said "You know what I realized after nine years? Ignorance is bliss." It is true in the sense that with ignorance there is nothing to do. You feel no obligation to anyone. Except when we choose this route, we will always be in bondage, and we can repeat this process again and again, until we choose to work on it.

It is freedom that we seek. Freedom from the tyranny of the ego which allows us to justify all the things that we do to protect this assumed boundary between ourselves and others. If we knew how deeply intertwined we are to each other we would not even think of harming another.

There will be no wars, no crimes committed. There will be peace.

But because there are as many desires in this world as there are humans, the world will go on as it does. We will have the same history, only the scenes change, that is if we don't annihilate each totally.

One person asked me why the Dalai Lama does not rally all the leaders in the world so that the Chinese government will give back Tibet. The answer is that he can not and will not interfere, by choice. His silence, the cultivation of peace within himself is a far greater contribution to humanity. This is not so easy to accept, but it is so.

To cultivate awareness, we have to do it from moment to moment. Simply be aware of your breath. It is what connects us to everyone and everything. Then you can ask yourself these things: "Who am I?" "What am I here for?"

Your first task is to remember who you are.

How to Develop Fearlessness

This is such a funny video. Please listen to it while reading the hub.

/watch?

I remember having to spank my only child one day when he was really little. I was crying on the inside while I was doing it but it needed to be done. It was for his own good.

I had to write a quite painful letter the other day. It was to cut off communications with someone I was, and still am, quite fond of. A beloved friend. I did not want to do it but it was necessary.

I had to examine why it was painful. It was because I had to confront my own emotions, the ones that I consider improper and not worthy of me. Not only am I vain, I am also spiritually materialistic. The paradox is that as one becomes spiritually materialistic, it is the same time that one becomes spiritually bankrupt.

There are feelings that we categorize as "not belonging" to a spiritually mature individual: jealousy, rage, envy, thoughts of vengeance, possessiveness. These are considered "bad" feelings.

To develop fearlessness is to confront that which we fear face to face.

This is what is painful. When one decides that it is time to sever one's relationship to rejecting these feelings as bad, a radical severance is required. It is painful to cut through frivolity because we want to hang on to it. It is our nature to want to do so.

Frivolity comes in many forms, not necessarily as simple as vanity paying so much attention to how one looks physically. It could take the form of greed in the sense of spiritual progress.

This is even more dangerous than simple vanity.

Just like an umbilical cord that needs to be cut, one has to have ruthless compassion towards oneself when using the Sword of Manjusri. Above all else, it requires absolute honesty with oneself, to accept rather than shove under the rug, to be able to say yes they are there, these feelings and that they do not necessarily diminish oneself.

These feelings are thoughts, fueled with emotions, but when we relate to them fully we find that just like everything else, they pass. To reject them is to empower them and to empower them is to not recognize the fact that like everything else, they are an avenue to freedom.

On the one hand, while it is painful to acknowledge these emotions, facing them with the Sword of Manjusri allows one to do the right thing for oneself- to realize that to progress on the path to freedom, one has to cut through frivolities, not of one's relationship with others but with oneself, and to transmute the fiery nature of emotions.

To become fearless is to reclaim authentic power and to know that everything, every event, every person that we meet, we created in order to usher us to absolute freedom.

We invited them there at the deepest level because in the more encompassing view, our objective is to realize that only our thoughts separate us from others.

So we acknowledge that the other person or event was not the cause of anger, it is rather oneself rejecting feelings as they come and questioning why they arise when one is supposed to be above them. We accept that we have them, we do not hang on to them, we do not act on them, rather we observe them. This is discriminating awareness.

And we give thanks for all that there was and hope that in some way we have enriched someone else's life if only for a short time, and that to let them grow, we have to respect their free will and honor their paths.

*Manjusri is the god of discriminating awareness. In the Buddhist literature, his flaming sword is the symbol of wisdom and ruthless compassion, the one that cuts through all duality, arrogance and frivolity.

How to do a Simple Visualization

I inserted the Zen relaxation video in the very beginning of this hub so that you can play it while you are reading the hub.

/watch?v

We are given five physical senses so that we may communicate to the physical world composed of solid, tangible and measurable form of matter.

The world that we live in is a product of the collective consciousness of the people in it. Yes, all 6 billion plus of us, creating thought, which moves energy, which then creates matter as we see it. The manifest.

I will not go into religion, or belief systems or political scenarios. I will confine this hub to a discussion on how to communicate properly what you wish to the unmanifest.

There are rules and they must be followed STRICTLY.

1. You can not covet that which belongs to another. You must not.

2. You must never influence the will of another. You must NEVER wish another harm.

3. You have to have faith..perfected faith..that if it is good for you, it will manifest. For a discussion of Faith, I suggest that you go to the Bible, the Hall of Faith.

There is nothing that someone owns that you can not have yourself if you sincerely desire it and if it is good for you in the long run. You can have what you want, in another form, another garment if you will.

The analogy being the computer at Starship Enterprise.

You order the computer to make a certain drink, and it gives it to you. Another officer does not have to have your drink because he can simply order one himself. This is very important.

For number 2, it applies directly to human relationships and romantic love. You formulate the

The reason being in that realm we go into the will of another and as long as you are bound to this, you are bound to disappointment. This is the meaning of "Be careful what you wish for, it might come true."

One person's prince/princess could be your source of pain. You let them go and you let it be. You do not have to go out seeking that person, you simply have to pay attention so that you will know when he or she arrives in your life.

With perfected faith, you have detachment. It is detachment from the outcome that you want. An example would be, you want flowers. Well you go into the backyard and you see that the lilies have bloomed. That is manifestation, simple and clear.

So we go into the process of how you go about it.

1. Relax..whatever it is that you do in order to relax do so.
2. Go into the list of your desires and choose ONE
3. Use all of your senses to get into the FEELING of having what you want.

a. What?
b. Look?
c. Taste?
d. Touch?
e. Smell?
f. Sound?

It is NOT watching a movie...it is BEING the movies.
Observe the difference. Know the difference.

Do not worry if you are not good at it in the beginning. With practice you will be good at it.

Lastly and the most important. Keep your desires to yourself until your faith is perfected. Keep doing the exercise.

How to Let Go of Everything, a Technique in Releasing

Once I met a man in one of the seminars I attended. He runs every morning before our sessions and when one time he hurt his leg on the course of our training I massaged it. During this time he had told me that his brother lives in a dumpster of a home and that his mother, a socialite in one of the big cities constantly begs him to please take care of his brother. He refused and continues to refuse. My logical mind could not fathom this, until a few days ago.

To enable someone to hang on to their addiction is to actually hinder them from their growth. It is what is termed as idiot compassion. The textbook definition of compassion.

Contrary to what our logical minds can conceive an addiction does not have to be with chemicals. An addiction is simply something that one has a compulsion to do, whether it be exercise, food, sex, the temporary ecstasy of drugs or or it could be hanging on to any identity that enables us to generate something out of our intended audience.

Real compassion is intelligent. It is sharp, ruthless, and most importantly, it comes from a space of unconditional love where there is no room for frivolity. The analogy being, would you give someone money when you know they would use it to buy drugs? It is the same with continuing to validate a belief by listening to them and commenting on something that they want to or unconsciously trying to validate.

Had the man in the story tried to "alleviate" his brother's condition, it would have hindered the brother from experiencing what he wanted to experience.

To continue in the path, we need to release all kinds of baggage. We travel light. But we also have to honor the stages in the path.

This release affirmation is a combination from several sources and I only formulated them here for simplicity. You can rearrange the words, delete or add words and phrases however it suits you. What is important, always, is what rings true to you.

Release technique "I release every thought pattern, attitude, behavior, programming, cultural and ancestral beliefs patterns, things and relationships that are longer conducive to my well being on the physical and spiritual level at this point in my path. I bless them all for at one time or another they were necessary for my growth. May they all be encased in divine light and divine love and returned to the Source."

So the steps of this technique:

On the spiritual level, we release everyone into the space of unconditional love. Say the release affirmation above every day. Pay attention to your feelings. Your feelings are your gauge, an inner guidance mechanism. If you always feel bad when you talk to someone because of anything, then perhaps it is time to let go of this relationship. You are not bound by anything. Only our minds try to cage us, but we are all free.

On the physical level, we let go of things that we don't use anymore and don't intend to use. Cleaning the closet, so to speak, but also drawers, cupboards, all the material things that someone else may use, we give to someone who can use them or donate to charity. Others we throw away.

The combination of the two allows for other experiences to come to our lives be they in the form of material things or new relationships.

How to Love Unconditionally

To begin to touch heaven, we must first relate to the earth.

No Master has ever denied the existence of the phenomenal world. To do so would be foolish. The earth is where we human beings are. It is here where we interact with each other, each interaction caused by our karmic connections from past lives.

We have to admit that this phenomenal world is fascinating. So many colors, so many textures, sight, sound, shapes, oh so much to explore, including the rise and flow of feelings for another person, which is the most vivid and most fascinating of it all:romantic love. So much so that history abounds with it and we love to read those stories of romantic love.

We get distracted and yet when we are able to relate to the earth as it is, we would have learned what Jesus Christ meant when he said "Be in the world but not of it." You are so much more than this phenomenal world and even the bible tells us "Don't you know that you are gods?"

There are no coincidences here; even meeting the person at the coffee shop where you get your coffee in the morning is not a chance meeting. Each meeting is a sacred contract.

There are rules that all religions tell us. Do not cheat, lie, steal, covet. Do not harm another. These rules are not arbitrary. The very simple reason, the truth is that every transgression against another is a karmic debt and each debt that we incur is repaid in full, if not in one lifetime then in the next. To some it may take many lifetimes.

The energetic cost to our soul in terms of evolution is much too much. It is really inner wisdom that propels us to do what is true to ourselves. We are all pure, perfect, unblemished.

The purpose of each interaction is to resolve these karmic issues. When we do not recognize this, we remain bound by ignorance and the consequence of ignorance is suffering. As humans we all have to turn the karmic wheel.

There is a way out of the karmic wheel. This is what the masters in every religion learn when they begin the path of meditation/contemplation/self inquiry.

After many years of discipline they can come back and begin to teach, but because they are free their actions are no longer karmically bound. When they go, it will be as if a bird has flown and only the wind carries the memory of the bird having been there. No traces left.

As human beings we feel love. We categorize this love according to our relationship with the other person but the feelings that we have are only a manifestation of the pure unconditional love that we have welling inside of us. Love is our gateway to freedom and as the Bible says, "For God so loved us all that He gave his only begotten son for our sins."

The sacrifice of the Son of God is only a symbol, no more. It is to say that God loves us all equally, including Jesus Christ, but Jesus Christ has already known that this is his role. And although the Bible tells us that He did show signs of human feelings as He was undergoing the persecution and crucifixion, He knew it beforehand and therefore played His role. Few people can understand Him as God so we have to relate to Him as the Son of God. A man.

When we feel romantic love towards another we know that that kind of love is sustainable only at the conscious level. A romantic relationship is sustained because the two people that are involved choose to stay. Because it is at the conscious level, we are in fact honoring our contracts, that which is required for us to repay our karmic debts, whether we like it or not.

We know that this is so because no matter how much we love your husband/wife/partner, there are times that we do not feel very loving towards them. They did or did not do something and that action or inaction hurt the human side of us or they have habits that we would rather they do not have. We expected something, and in our minds, they disappointed us.

Real love is unconditional. This means, without conditions attached to it. It is only our limited minds, a part of our ego, that want us to own/be with/be part of/control another person.

The love that Jesus Christ represents, what the Masters call Cosmic/Universal love, is like the sun shining on everyone.

It does not distinguish between sinner or saint, pauper or prince, someone who is as innocent as a child, or a hardened criminal.

The sun shines on both the sinner and saint. It has no expectation of return and therefore only benefits the giver. It is all encompassing and unassuming, like a well which when opened becomes an oasis. Eventually, this oasis becomes an ocean.

When we are able to relate to this and see that there is only ebb and flow of feelings brought by our minds, then we can relate to the statement "To be in the world but not of it."

To be in the world, enjoy it, see it as it is, and know that it is all a fascinating play. It is here where we not only participate because we chose to,but also that which we require as a classroom to learn our lessons.

Then we go back and see that the suffering associated with that limited romantic love was necessary for our growth. It was a part of our path, a gateway, which when entered into shows us how really narrow our former perspective was. There are no distinctions when we love. We love, that is all.

And we see the humor as we remember our seven year old son asking us which one we love more, him or the dog?

How to Merge Magic, Myth and Reality

I was thinking of the Tower of Babel and the reason in the Bible why there are so many languages today. I think the reason God created many languages is for the people to appreciate contrasts.

If I were to envision a conceited God, I would say He created the different languages so that He can be serenaded in different languages. But I can not comprehend the mind of God so I will not go there.

At any rate I can not imagine a conceited God.

When two people can communicate without the use of language, we enter into the realm of magic and myth, and yet, it is entirely possible. It is real. Studies of twins separated at birth have documented this.

In the world of myth and magic, the unseen, a soul is born with a twin, hence the term "Soul Mate". I take this to mean a soul separated from its twin at birth. There are many movies about this.

It is possible for two people to communicate with each other without the filter of the ego. When this happens that communication becomes a dance. It is beautiful but it is also scary, in the sense that there is no place to hide. One is totally exposed, vulnerable, naked, no room for hypocrisy.

This is the kind of communication between a guru and a disciple, when the student is ready to be totally exposed, vulnerable. The paradox is that this is the exact state in which the guru is also able to transmit the best. The student, by accepting himself, as he is, unmasked, totally naked, can now realize that he and the guru are the same. The separation is only in his mind.

But what if the relationship is not between a guru and a student, in the formal sense? This is where it gets tricky. One who is able to read another's thought is so very tempted to do it all the time, with everybody. An ego enhancement tool . It is one of the six yogic powers that come when the mind is quieted [See the Yoga Sutras of Patanjali]

We all have these thoughts that we do not want to share with others. They are too private, shameful to have or entertain since they are so "off" the spiritual path. So we think. Thinking is the ego's tool to take us away from the present, the dharma experienced as tantra.

It takes discipline not to invade someone's thoughts without his or her permission and hence all of the sages warn about it. Like a drug, it can intoxicate and when one indulges in it, the person now becomes a drunken monkey.

On the other hand, if it is between two people who wish to do it, voluntarily, then it becomes a beautiful dance. No ego involved, a free flow, freedom instead of a cage.

This kind of communication exists between a parent and a child. They are in tune with each other.

In the romantic sense, when one is fortunate to find that person who is his/her twin flame, and both are willing to be vulnerable, the meeting of two minds merge myth, magic, and reality. No need for words.

What do you have to do when you find this person? Be fearless. The paradox is that when you are most vulnerable, you are also the strongest. Why? Because the soul that was split has now become whole and you will know it beyond the shadow of a doubt.

How to Reclaim Your Own Innate Power

I have only worked with two long term clients as a coach. By long term I mean one hour every week for more than 12 months. The results of those coaching sessions are so remarkable that I will share them with you. In both instances, as a coach, I am not allowed to dictate what the clients have to do.

To dictate is to dis-empower if not to unempower. Always choose to empower another for in so doing, you empower yourself in more ways than the limited mind can create.

In our sessions I only showed them how to change a way of thinking so that eventually they realized that they create everything in their lives.

No outside force. The important thing is to "FEEL" the difference between attributing an outside circumstance as the cause of our predicament and taking responsibility for whatever occurred.

Here is a transcript, abridged, on one of those sessions:

Observe the difference between the following sentences:

1. "My wife makes me mad."

2. "I allowed myself to be upset by what my wife said to me."

Now "FEEL" the difference between the two sentences.
1. "My boss fired me."

2. "Subconsciously, I wanted to leave that job. I did not love my job, I was staying there to put food on the table but I realized that that job is not the only thing I can do so having to leave that job was a blessing, although it did not feel like it at that time."

Behind every word is a thought. The word is a vehicle, no more. However since we are so thoroughly indoctrinated in a habitual thought pattern we are not even aware of it, we have to do it the other way around.

Say the words, feel the words and know the new thought pattern it has created.

Here are common exercises. Finish each sentence as you please

I don't want to
I prefer to
I would like to
I choose to
I would rather
I intend to
I probably can
I can and I will

A few key points. Words are vehicles. They are created from thought. We are accustomed to thinking a certain way so we need to change a pattern of thinking by playing with the words, which creates a new thought pattern and with it a certain feeling. It is by feelings that we communicate to the universe.

You can not request the universe for a home on the beach in La Jolla if in the back of your mind you are thinking "Oh, but how am I going to regenerate the 8 figures required to afford a home there?

Answer, if you had it before you can have it again. No doubt." Get the picture?

Wish you everything that will make you happy. Oops..other way around, be happy, then you can have everything.

How to Relate to Money

Money is a sensitive topic to almost everyone. As I write only by experience, I had to go to the depths of my perception of money in order to get here, to this article.

So I will begin with this story. I did not originate it but I am using it as a tool to illustrate a point.

A long time ago, in a kingdom far far away a King got tired of his long time Queen. Oh there are so many young and beautiful princesses who would jump at the chance to be queen. He could have as many concubines as he wanted but there can only be one queen.

The Queen, although older, is still beautiful in form but also a wise one. She knew of her husband's restlessness and knows full well that it will pass. The king was so enamored with a young and beautiful princess who would not let him make her a concubine.

She wanted to be queen so she told the king that her price was the Queen's crown. The king wanted this princess and so foolishly, he wanted to get rid of the Queen who had been with him through all times. Indeed there was no one more faithful, kind, and wise and had it not been for her wise advice, he would have lost the kingdom many times over. Still he forgot. He wanted the young and beautiful princess.

Although in his heart he still loved the queen, the King thought, oh she is so old and my sons will be very happy to have her in their own castles and I can live with my young queen forever. He thought of the best way to get rid of the old Queen was to offer her half the Kingdom if she wanted. A small price to pay. He was more than rich, his descendants and the people would be more than provided for. The palace coffers were full.

So one night the king told the queen "I am in love with this beautiful young Princess, and I want to make her Queen. I wish you to leave the palace and go and live with one of our sons. Half the kingdom is yours and you are welcome to take anything from the Palace as you desire, and he ordered the scribes to write it as his proclamation.

When I wake up in the morning, I shall declare to the people that you have abdicated your crown and I shall proclaim the new queen and he left to spend the night in another room, delighted that he would have a new Queen the following morning."

At midnight, he was awakened from his sleep for he felt the bed move! When he opened his eyes, he saw that the strongest men in the palace were carrying him out of the palace! Furious, he demanded an explanation at which time the Queen appeared.

And she said "O King, according to your words last night which you proclaimed an order last night, I am allowed to take anything from the palace that I desire. I desire no gold, no more than the clothes that I am wearing and a few other belongings, but when I married you, I gave you my heart and it is what I desire back the most, for no riches, no glory, no title shall take the place of my love for you. Therefore I decided it is you I will take with me when I leave the palace."

The King realized how foolish he had been and begged the Queen for forgiveness. And they grew old together. And the kingdom flourished even more.

I have never been tempted with money so I cannot tell you what I would do if it were to happen. I do know that I resented the unwritten caste system in the Philippines that pegs people into categories according to their economic status. Money is a means, no more.

On the other hand, a long time ago, I could have been tempted with both fame and power until I knew what power is. In the story, I would have been the young Princess when I was young but now I am old and know better.

So now that that is done and over with, let us discuss how you can change the way you look at money.

First, wealth is a state of mind. In the story the Queen will always be queen regardless of what she has and she knew it. You need to think about this. Who you are inside is not defined by the outside circumstances in your life. A simple truth: To have something, anything, you have to want it.

Second, you have your own combination of unique talents that you can use to create what it is that you want. Your task is to define that combination of talents and use them to create the money that you want. It is the other way around. First define what you want in terms of lifestyle then, you create the circumstances that will allow you that lifestyle.

You might find that you do not necessarily need to have a lot of money to have that lifestyle.

Third, you follow your thoughts and ideas with action.
Fourth you joy every moment in the journey.

Exercises:[Note: These are a few methods which I have used with my coaching clients. One couple acquired a 17 acre piece of property after simply defining what they wanted. Another person bought the home of his dreams. It takes discipline to do it but it works]

1. Take the largest bill with you window shopping and decide "Oh look at those shoes on sale for x amount of money. If I WANTED, I could buy it."

2. Give to some cause that you feel strongly about, or to someone who cannot give back to you.

3. Find out where your money goes and reallocate it to have the following: You will need identical containers labeled with the following. You will need to put coins in every container every day for 40 days. If you miss one day, you have to start all over again.

a. Charity. You cannot give what you don't already have. When you give to someone who cannot give back it means you are more than rich enough to give. Now, a caveat. Please do not give unless your heart tells you to do so. It is better not to give if in so doing you will feel poor. When you give the feeling should be I am happy I am able to give.

b. Savings. Only to the extent that it will discipline you into putting something away and you will see the balance increase every month. This is what the banks need to see when you want to make a major purchase such as a house, an apartment complex, etc.

c. Necessities. You need this for food, shelter, gas, insurance, your child's summer camp.

d. Investment. Long term wealth requires that you do some kind of investment. You decide this for yourself.

e. Education. You need to constantly educate yourself about wealth. Study wealth. Study the people who have accumulated it.

f. Travel. To expand your horizons, meet other people.

g. My one heart's desire. It does not matter what it is. An Aston Martin? A Bulgari necklace? A Chalet in Switzerland? You have to put yourself in the state of having it and this will remind you of it.

h. For the child within something that will make you happy immediately.

4. Find out how you can have multiple sources of income. Use your specific talents and skills to do something that will reward you not only with satisfaction but also monetarily
5. Be happy with where you are and then build from there. This is what gratitude is about. The fact that you are reading this is already something to be happy about.

6. Above all else, be kind to yourself. Know that every challenge that you face, including financial challenge is an avenue to self development. I know this as truth.

How to Release Past Experiences That Are No Longer Serving You

It is not easy to let go of the past. We somehow feel anchored to them, they give us an identity that is much easier to hang on to than to release.

I had clients who, in the beginning, were not able to transcend childhood trauma for a long time. Change can only come from within. It cannot be enforced.

I can not relate to the traumas but I have found that this ritual works for both childhood trauma and broken hearts.

You can do this at any time, anywhere. You simply need a place where you can do the exercise and not be disturbed. Yes, even in the bathroom but No, not while driving or operating heavy machinery.

Close your eyes. Find yourself in a dark hallway where at the very end there is a door that has light seeping in from the outside. As you go through the hallway, you hear the sound of doors closing behind you.

The doors represent something that you need to leave behind.

An abusive childhood, an abusive lover..etc etc..You can have as many doors closing behind you as you like.

You walk, not afraid, because you see that at the end of the hallway is this door with light coming from the outside and you are confident that there is something wonderful that awaits when you open the door.

You do not hurry because it takes time for the other doors to close behind you.

As you reach the end of the hallway and open the very last door, your eyes needed to adjust to the sunlight and when you have, you see that right in front of you is a beautiful, beautiful garden, with all the plants you have ever loved! The flowers of the season are in full bloom!

You look further and you see there is a natural waterfalls where the garden was built, and there is a natural pool, not too deep and not too shallow. You cup your hands and taste the water and it is sweet.

You look at your reflection in the water and you find yourself as you have always imagined you would look, full of beauty, full of strength, full of life, full of happiness and you figure out that this water is magical. It is inviting you to go in.

You dip your toe in the water and find its temperature most perfect. You take off your clothes and soak in the pool. The water is removing every pain, every bruise, every emotional baggage that you carry.

You stay a while, feeling that the water seeps into every cell of your body and removing every painful memory from them. .

They no longer serve you and you need to release them into the healing water where it is transformed into an elixir instead.

Your cells are renewed and in place of the painful memories, the imprint of unconditional love has been placed instead.

When you have felt cleansed and are ready to go,you look at the clothes and they are now shimmering white, clean and ohhh so soft.

A group of fairies were cleansing it while you were taking your bath.

You put on your clothes, follow the other path that leads away from the pool and out of the garden. Behold, you see your home! As you were on the last step out of the garden, Merlin appears and hands you a stone [this can be anything that you hold dear to your heart and you associate with what is possible.

A piece of jewelry, a memento from someone you loved and who loved you unconditionally, a symbol of unconditional love, something that holds meaning for you] and he tells you that that stone is your portal to the magical garden.

Your instruction is to rub that stone every time you wish to enter your magical garden.

You can always come back to your magical garden anytime, anywhere. You simply have to be present, this moment.

How to Shift Your Mood

I love the series "Dune" and "Children of Dune". I don't remember how many times I have watched them but I have watched them a lot. Of course it is not the same as reading the book, but for what the director had to work with to make the film, he did a fantastic job. Now I am waiting for Steven Spielberg to make the movie "David the King".

In Dune, there was a scene where Paul Atreides was training with Gurney and because Paul had just been tested in the black box by the Reverend Mother Helen Mohiam of the Bene Gesserit, he was not focused on the training.

Had he been in a real combat, he would have been wounded. He dismissed it as "I'm not in the mood" and Gurney answers "Not in the mood? Mood is for women and children, young pup. Mood isn't for fighting" It is true. Mood is not for fighting but we all go through different moods during the day. It is not confined to women and children. There are so many graduations in this "mood"

For this exercise, you will learn how to shift your mood.

You need to pay attention to how you feel. How do you feel right now?Acknowledge that you are feeling down (if you are) and then move on to do the following exercise

We begin with whatever was right in front of us..a book, a candle holder, a pencil..whatever is right in front of you.

In order to truly appreciate that thing, you need to hold it in your hand, feel it, observe it, be at one with it.

Appreciation takes time and when you do give yourself a chance to have this time to appreciate anything, you will soon realize that for that thing to get there in your hand, right at this moment, this lowly pencil or pen, countless man-hours were expended.

To get the pen into your hand was a product of the work and coordination of a lot of people.

Now you move on to another thing and so on and so on. Look around you!

As you do this, the worry/anxiety/anger/ will dissipate and be replaced with wonder. The key is not to hurry and pay attention to your feelings..you need to move on from a "down feeling" to "neutral" to "appreciative" to "happy". There are countless stages in between.

The key is not denying how you are feeling. It is acknowledging it, and moving forward regardless of the circumstance. This requires discipline: the discipline of focus, and the discipline of patience. Focus on what you have right now, not in the past.

How do you feel right now, after doing the exercise? Exactly.

Mood or feeling is how we communicate with the universe. Feelings is a combination of thought and energy. We think the thought- it is a conscious process- and a mood is created, but the resulting feeling is much more powerful than the thought. You can feel it in your body.

When you are angry or sad, there is a different set of chemical reactions that occur. When you are happy another set of chemical reactions occur. There are different receptors in your brain for each process. The important thing is to know that a negative feeling triggers a set of chemical reactions that are not good for your body.

Some of us are so accustomed to thinking negatively we don't even notice it until we actually pay attention to it.

We need to lessen the gaps between happy emotions in order for our desires to come faster.

How To Write Love Letters

The heart speaks a language which no words can capture. The words approximate the feelings but they are not the same.

Knowing this, we begin by saying that a love letter is a letter written to approximate a feeling which you wish to express to another person, and something that that person can always go back to. To fully express that feeling you have to be with the other person whose feelings match yours.

And yet, love letters mean so much. Because there is always a part of you that is carried with a handwritten letter. Writing a letter by hand is a lost art, and therefore, any letter written by hand is precious.

When I was really young I remember a movie called Love Letters. It was a film about two people who broke up and each wanted to get back the letters each wrote to each other. The question who owns the letters?

There is a song by the Lettermen called Love Letters and I will only quote the lines which mean most to me

"Love letters straight from your heart keeps us so near while apart"

"I memorized every line. I kissed the name that you signed. And darling then I'll read again right from the start. Love letters straight from your heart."

I don't know how to write letters anymore. Sometimes I have a hard time reading my own handwriting! The email is so much easier and faster, and besides, the email does not show how long it took us to write it.

All letters come from the heart. One has to appreciate the feel of the pen and the linen paper. There is a ritual that comes with it. You have to take out your pens, decide which one to use,

take out the box of linen, decide which one to use, in contrast to just sitting in front of the computer and typing away.

I used to exchange letters with someone a long time ago. They were not love letters per se, just a correspondence between long term friends.

He studied calligraphy and I had kept his letters for a long time but decided there were too many personal things in his letters that I would rather not share with anyone, so I destroyed all of them when I moved.

We had lost touch and he simply did not want to communicate with me by email so if I want to hear whether he is in Brazil at the Carnival or in Siguatepec or somewhere in the Carribean, I have to write him by hand.

He demands it and expects it. In fact, he told me so in the last email "What happened to us? We used to write each other." He meant by hand. Oh, but I have nothing exciting to write about my life! So how can I write? What would I write about?

The last time I wrote a personal letter it took me almost four hours and several discarded linen sheets and now I remember why as I opened my journal and think about it.

A letter, written by hand is so immediate, so demanding of you to confront your thoughts and feelings and in a way so scary. Every letter carries with it a part of you. An email can be erased by simply hitting the delete button.

A handwritten note, a letter is semi permanent. It cannot be undone. It is a record of someone's thoughts and feelings at the time it was written.

And this is exactly why my friend who travels a lot, demands it. He is after all who he is. And he has a right to do so, because no matter how busy he is and no matter where he goes, he always writes back, by hand.

And so how do you write a love letter? You write what is in your heart and you do not go back and edit the letter because sending that letter means an implicit, immediate, and titanic trust with the person you are sending it to. Trust being a solid foundation of romantic love.

How to Write Your Own Life Script/Affirmations

If you were hungry and I offered you food to eat, you have the option to take the food or not.This is the power of choice. I can force feed you, but you will still have to digest the food to nourish your body. The same is true with the soul.

One can give you affirmations but they have to ring true for you. The best way therefore is for you to create your own affirmations.

In this article I have compiled words so that you can make your own sentences, but the purpose of the exercise is really so you can make your own so by all means, be creative.

I suggest that you print this out and then using a colored marker, mark the words that ring true for you and then formulate the sentence at the end.

Introductory phrases
From my heart and with everything that I AM
In Divine love everything that I need
For highest will and good of all concerned
In full alignment with divine purpose my life purpose
my soul purpose

Introductory phrases
From my heart and with everything that I AM
Divine love everything that I need
for highest will and good of all concerned
in full alignment with divine purpose my life purpose
my soul purpose

Actions
Surround me with
I intend
I invite
I accept
I ask
Release/Transcend
Be done now
Done with
Energy patterns
Be released from
Transcend
Fully committed
Search for and erase
Search for and replace
Search for and remove Seek for
Search for
Root out
Completely eliminate
Fully manifest merge
To struggle

Intend to totally
I manifest
I accept
I embrace
I am fully in tune with

Nouns/objects Physical Material Spiritual Beliefs Attitudes Memories
God
Energies
Energy channels
Energy bodies
Soul creation
Divine Self
Dimensions
Existencies

Universes
Soul creation and birth
Unconditional love
Teachers
Healers
Guides
Mentor
Divine light
Divine love
Blockages
Mindsets
Attitudes
Behaviors Karma
Karmic council
Cells

Sample Sentences
Introductory phrase then action then object
Examples:
From my heart and with everything that I AM, I ask (your own personal choice of being) to surround me with light and love and illuminate my path.

If it is for my highest good, then I manifest NOW. I ask the universe to help me in this process and it is done.

I now intend and choose to transcend all of which in the past have prevented me from living a happy, joyful and abundant life

If it is for my highest good, then I manifest NOW. I ask the universe to help me in this process and it is done

I now intend and choose to transcend all of the experiences which in the past have prevented me from living a happy, joyful and abundant life

I am now living a life in full alignment with my divine soul purpose.

Of Koans and Mantras

This article will touch on Koans and Mantras as tools for arriving at the space of unmanifest.

One of the most famous koans is "What is the sound of one hand clapping?"

From Wikipedia, and this meaning approximates the meaning of the koan in the East..." A Koan consists of a story, dialogue, question, or statement whose meaning cannot be accessed by rational thinking, yet it may be accessible by intuition"

A Zen Master gives the student a koan as a tool to arrive at a state of being-ness. Sometimes it takes years to solve one koan.

The answer is neither logical nor illogical. It is a measure of the state of mind of the student. This state of mind is what the Zen master pays attention to when the student comes to him to present his solution.

It follows that two students given the same koan will give different answers. The answer does not have to be a lengthy explanation, sometimes it is an action, a grunt, or silence.

The object of the koan is to quiet the mind which is normally so full of thoughts. Exhaust the logical thinking mind and in so doing arrive at the place, without thought. This is the place of the unmanifest. It is also the place/space we want to access when we earnestly desire for something material.

In several religious traditions mantras are used instead of koans. The objective is the same. There is an excellent book by Eknath Easwaran called "The Mantram Handbook"

In it he outlines only the most popular ones for different religions. When a mantram is incorporated into the being of the person, his mind is quieted. It is in this space where creation occurs.

We normally do this in the popular culture using visualization/affirmation techniques. Strictly speaking, these are techniques/tools to "bridge" the gap between the conscious and the subconscious. It is the subconscious that does the work.

One can create his own mantram. For example, one can use "Hail Mary" or "Hare Krishna" or "Om" or "Ram" or "Kyrie Eleison" . In fact the name of God in different languages is sufficient. You can choose yours.

Caution: It is possible to "get lost" while doing the mantrams and koans so it is advisable to use these techniques only when you are in a safe place and there is no demand for your attention. It is not advisable to do this while driving or operating heavy machinery.

The paradox is that when we arrive at this space, there is absolute peace and there is nothing to be desired except union with God.

All the other material desires vanish.

Note: mantrams and mantras are used interchangeably in the literature

Seven day Simple Meditations

Clearing the Path: Simple Meditations

I write only from experience and I write only when I am moved to it. It took me six months to simply go with the flow...this was not as easy as you would think. I am used to a very rigid schedule. I used to plan everything.

It turns out that our inner guidance system, when we really listen to it, is infinitely better than the logical thinking mind. But even for me, knowing it intellectually is not enough. I had to experience it. By the experience, your faith is solidified.

One has to experience it. It is not an intellectual exercise. We are not trying to experience the state of bliss. We are simply trying to be in the moment.

You have to both bite and chew the food before you swallow it. Then you will have to digest it. No one else can do it for you.

If you have been meditating for a while, that is wonderful. You may or may not want to do this exercise

This is mostly for beginners who would like to start in the art of listening to their inner voice.

For us to appreciate music, hear the subtleties of the notes and be moved by them to tears of joy, we have to listen to the music in silence.

The same is true with our inner guidance. It is always there. Call it intuition if you will, but it is an inner compass that will tell us the course of action to take. It is never wrong. The logical thinking mind may tell you otherwise but that is exactly its function.

There are so many sounds, inner dialogues that we have to silence for this to happen so we begin the process by doing one meditation/contemplation per day.

Just the attempt to do it is enough. No need to be hard on yourself. If you remember to do the exercise during the day, fine. If not, move on. Do not let this exercise be a part of something you have to do.

So here it goes: I only numbered them for easy reference. I would suggest that you print it out

One Lesson One for Each day of the Week: Write each lesson on a 3x5 card or any size card that would allow you to carry it and look at it once in a while. Pull one card randomly for the day, then meditate/contemplate on that particular lesson during the day. You do not have to do them in any particular order.
It is remembering to do it sometime during the day that is important.

1. Forgiveness

Thought: Forgiveness
Word: As I forgive, I am also forgiven.
Action: Mentally forgive everyone whom you think has done you wrong in the past. Forgive yourself for what you think you have done wrong unto others.
Better yet, when you have time, write their names on one sheet then shred the sheet or if you can burn the sheet. No one has to see the sheet but you so go all out for it.

2. Release

Thought: Release

Word: "I release every thought pattern, attitude, imprint, behavior, programming, cultural and ancestral beliefs, things and relationships that are longer conducive to my well being on the physical and spiritual level at this point in my path.
I am grateful for them all. I bless them all for at one time or another they were necessary for my growth. May they all be encased in divine light and divine love and returned to the Source.

Action: Take something from your home that you are no longer using and give it away or throw it away.

3. Gratitude

Thought: Gratitude
Word: I am grateful for every breath I take.
Action: Feel happy for anything in your life that makes you happy. A loved one, a pet, your car, a blossom in the garden, your new herb garden...you get the idea.

4. Creativity

Thought: Creativity
Word: I feel highly creative and in tune with the world.
Action: Discover a hidden talent. Do something you have never done before.

5. Boundless Love

Thought: Unconditional Love
Word: As I love unconditionally, so I am loved.
Action: Hug someone you love for a little while longer than normal. Tell them you love them while looking at their eyes and feeling this love between the two of you. It can be your pet.

6. Loving myself

Thought: Loving myself
Word: I am a product of love. The more I access this love for myself the more I am able to love others.
Action: Look at yourself in the mirror, look at your eyes and say the words out loud. I love you.

7. Connecting to the Source/God

Thought: God/Source
Word: I am connected to God/Source
Action: Anything that will allow you to connect...

You may create your own and add it to the deck if you feel like it.

At the end of the day, congratulate yourself for at least remembering to do the exercise even if you only did it once during the day.

I wish you love, and I wish you peace.

The Zero Step in the Manifestation Process

I manage a club both on Facebook called Manifesting Magical Moments

This is my latest post in the clubs and I thought I would share it with everyone.

The basic assumption that I have been making ever since I started the club is that everyone's self esteem is high enough that you all feel worthy of manifesting your desires. I have come to realize that even with the brightest and most successful people I have met, there is a tinge of "un-self worthiness". This is not so obvious.

We try to bury this as the "secret" side of us. Even I realized this in myself, looking back at my life. This inner feeling of "unworthiness" can be buried so deep, it manifests as guilt and shame. Guilt for many reasons, shame for many reasons. Some for things we did, some for things we did not do.

We have to let go of all of this junk from our consciousness in order to manifest our desires.

I know only a few people who have not exhibited these feelings. They are all happy with everything in their lives. One has been married forever and the other just found her true love, a prince through and through.

So how do we go about re-asserting our inner self worth? It is not easy to undo years of conditioning so we do the least invasive of all techniques. Of course, I will always recommend that you meditate but if your heart is not in it, then don't do it.

One of the absolute musts in my coaching sessions is the mirror technique. I have my clients look into their eyes in the mirror and tell themselves "I love you, [their name].

In the beginning a dozen times a day and as the days progress, for longer periods and for a greater number of times, until they actually FEEL that they accept everything about themselves. I mean everything

The good, the not so good, the serious and the funny. If they told me they did not do the exercise for the day we were supposed to have a session, I cancelled the session. It is as simple as that. It would have been a waste of their time and mine.

I know what it is to be judgmental. I was my own harshest critic.

I admit to having been harsher on myself than on anyone else. My coaching instructor and my friends in the coaching classes pointed this out to me. I was not aware of it, until they actually repeated my words to me and I realized, oh, it is true! As long as we do not feel deserving of what it is that we want, it cannot materialize.

Here is a short story to illustrate my point.

Once a lady met a prince. She did not know he was a prince since he was dressed in rags when they met. They married. She found out he was a prince when he took her to his castle after they were married! The lady could not believe she is now a princess. While she believed in fairy tales, she did not think it could happen to her! Why her? She was so ordinary was what she thought.

Within a few years, the prince fell in love with another and the lady had to leave the prince's castle and had to deal with the harsh realities of life after leaving the castle.

After many years the lady realized that it was all her thinking, and that deep within she did not believe she deserved to marry a prince, for after all, she was just an ordinary person.

She began to study herself and began to believe that she was special after all! She began to believe in herself and to feel worthy of everything that will make her happy. And then a miracle. The princess woke up! It was just a dream. The prince was by her side after all and she was still the princess she was meant to be.

I could have changed the story to reflect a man who finds oil in his backyard, or someone who invents something that can be used by anyone, or someone who just has a business that seems to soar. How long will you stay there?

Are you still in the dream or have you just been awakened? You are absolutely worth everything that you desire, and more. After all, YOU are the source of it all.

Go buy a pocket mirror and do the exercise of looking into your eyes and saying "I love you [say your name]. You deserve to be happy and fulfilled." How long and how often? Until you actually FEEL it. Minimum of 40 days for it to be ingrained within you.

A caveat: the feeling of unworthiness comes back when you are not aware of it, so carry the mirror with you at all times.

I end with a card given to me by a friend when I was twelve years old.

"May your life be filled with much happiness and only enough sorrow for you to know the difference."

Sincerely yours,
Melinda

Post Script

"Without a serene, pure, and firm heart, the truth cannot be grasped directly as it is. A brilliant intellect may discourse about it, as to its realization a disciplined mind is required." ~In "Essays in Zen Buddhism" by Daizets Teitaro Suzuki

There are many men and women who contributed to the development of this work either direcly or indirectly, by inspiration and by setting an example.

It is not possible to recreate here the library of the current author, however I would like to mention a few whose works I went back to, again and again during the course of my own self inquiry.

The author read the books by the following authors:

Chogyam Trungpa
Osho
Ram Dass
Shunryu Suzuki
Daizets Teitaro Suzuki
Thomas Merton
Eknath Iswaran
Ayn Rand
Thomas Merton
Richard Bach
Alan Watts
Ashvagosha Yogananda, Ramana Maharshi

About the Author

Melinda was born, raised, and educated in the Philippines, and came to the USA to pursue post graduate education.

After obtaining her Masters and Ph.D. degrees, and after doing Postdoctoral research, she worked as a Professor of Chemisty for several years.

Both as a student and as a professor, Melinda was a recipient of many scholarships/awards/grants and in addition Melinda was mentored by many generous men and women during her career.

Melinda is an author of articles in peer reviewed scientific journals. As a professor she has mentored students who have gone on to careers in the medical fields, chemistry and other science related fields as well as business and technology.

After leaving the academia, Melinda published a book entitled "My Journey to an Integrated Life."

Melinda also published several articles on popular online magazines.

In her life, Melinda has seen the never ending circle of life. Sometimes we give, sometimes we receive, sometimes we comfort others, sometimes we are comforted.

Melinda recognizes that while it is true that there is suffering in this world, there is also the beautiful human heart which sees that in every human interaction, be it with nature or with other human beings, there is hope and there is love. A fearless heart embraces all of it: The suffering and the alleviation of suffering both our own and that of others, in the pursuit of our own humanity, we find that we are all the same.

We only have to pay attention to discover our fearless hearts.

Melinda currently serves as President of Fearless Hearts Foundation and can be reached at

About the Author

email : info@fearlessheartsfoundation.org

For more information on Fearless Hearts Foundation, please visit the website at
www.fearlessheartsfoundation.org

Creed of the Fearless Hearts

I would be true, for there are those who trust me; I would be pure, for there are those who care; I would be strong, for there is much to suffer; I would be brave, for there is much to dare; I would be friend of all-the foe, the friendless; I would be giving, and forget the gift; I would be humble, for I know my weakness; I would look up, and laugh, and love and lift. I would be faithful through each passing moment. I would be constantly in touch with God; I would be strong to follow where I lead me; I would have faith to keep the path Christ trod. Who is so low that I am not his brother? Who is so high that I've no path to him? Who is so poor? I can not feel his hunger? Who is so rich I may not pity him? Who is so hurt I can not know his heartache? Who sings for joy my heart may never share? Who in God's heav'n has passed beyond my vision? Who to hell's depths where I may never fare? May None, then, call me for understanding. May none, then, turn to me for help in pain, and drain alone his bitter cup of sorrow, or find he knocks upon my heart in vain.

Adapted from
My Creed and Other Poems, ~ Howard Arnold Walter, 1912

www.ingramcontent.com/pod-product-compliance
Lightning Source LLC
LaVergne TN
LVHW090944080826
845145LV00003B/886

* 9 7 8 0 9 7 9 6 5 0 7 1 0 *